westland ltd

I0149700

HOW TO GET MARRIED IN NINE WEEKS

Rajat Banerjee has been working in the corporate real estate sector for the last fifteen years and, apart from real estate, has varied interests – in writing, theatre, movies, public speaking, and training.

Since passing out from IIT Roorkee, writing has been a passion with Rajat and he has penned down many ideas and stories, yet to published. This is his first self-help book.

He is presently based out of Hong Kong and travels to Delhi every few months along with his wife and son.

HOW TO GET MARRIED IN NINE WEEKS

The Key to Finding and Keeping the Ideal Life-partner

Rajat Banerjee

𝓦
Westland Ltd

westland ltd
61 Silverline Building, 2nd floor, Alapakkam Main Road, Maduravoyal, Chennai 600095
No. 38/10 (New No.5), Raghava Nagar, New Timber Yard Layout, Bangalore 560026
93, 1st Floor, Sham Lal Road, New Delhi 110002

First published in India by westland ltd 2014
Copyright © by Rajat Banerjee 2014

All rights reserved
10 9 8 7 6 5 4 3 2 1

ISBN: 978-93-84030-00-1

Typeset by Ram Das Lal

Contents

Introduction

Over the last few years, I have come across a number of young, smart people who are finding it increasingly difficult to get married. Amongst them are my friends, colleagues and acquaintances. And this situation is not for want of trying on their part. In fact, having watched them go about their lives, I have sensed their deep desire for a life-partner.

As I observed, I realised that as people approached their late twenties and early thirties, they seemed to grow in every aspect of their lives in terms of work experience, wealth, hobbies and friend circle, except in their ability to find a spouse. I saw some get quite close to doing so, but due to one reason or another, fall short of getting married.

So, it set me thinking. Why was it that in today's environment, with all the possible communication tools at our beck and call, are they still unable to find a suitable life-partner? After all, I found my life-partner even before cell phones were around!

I could not find an easy answer.

Was it because we had become too choosy about what we wanted?

Or, were we waiting for that absolutely perfect person to come along and sweep us off our feet?

In short, were we being unrealistic in our expectations?

Or was it a case of an overdose of the communication systems, which, instead of enhancing human interaction was in fact reducing it?

Was it pure coincidence that the right person did not materialise?

Or was it due to lack of effort either on the part of the person or the person's parents?

None of the above seemed to apply to the people I knew. They all appeared to have a balanced view of life, were quite realistic in their expectations and they all seemed to have tried reasonably hard to get married. So what was the problem? As mentioned earlier, I could not find an easy answer. Maybe it was a combination of some of the above factors coupled with other things which I am not aware of. Maybe it was destiny or maybe just something beyond our comprehension.

Then a thought flashed through my mind that maybe, and I say, *maybe,* these people should have conducted themselves differently in particular situations. This made me think that there *could* be some generic things that people who were trying to get married could do which might help them achieve their goal. I had been reading a variety of self-help books for the last three years and realised some of the fundamental things I had picked up from them could help people in their quest for a perfect partner.

One night, I awoke at about three am after which I could not go back to sleep. I lay in bed till four am and finally sat up, opened my BlackBerry notes and typed in the nine chapters that you see here in Section 1. It was very quiet at that hour and somehow my thoughts just flowed. All of a sudden, I saw things with a kind of clarity that is possible only in these rare moments and I decided I would write this book in the format you now hold. From that day it took me about four months to write this and about two more months to fine-tune it.

One of the questions that bothered me for some time was this: What qualified *me* to write this book? I was not trying to get married (I am happily married to the most wonderful woman I have ever met!). Neither did I dabble in trying to get people married and nor was I some sort of an motivational guru!

I figured there were a few reasons, given below, that gave me the legitimacy to write this book. Like I said earlier, I am happily married and all the credit for it goes to my wife who, to my mind, is one of those rare people who have an innate goodness about them. She has taught me a lot just by being the way she is and many of the things I have learned from her and our relationship have inadvertently found their way into this book.

I have a fair number of friends all over the country, from different walks of life and have spent a lot of time listening to them talk about their relationships. I would like to take this opportunity to thank each and every one of them for the invaluable insights they have provided me on the subject, as their experiences also form the basis of this book.

In a previous stint I was a personality trainer for a well-known franchise. I worked with approximately five hundred people across the country in various roles and courses, and it was during this time that I learnt a lot about people and what made them tick. I realised that sometimes we have the ability to say something which can impact a few and provide them with results that are amazing.

To sum up, if this book makes sense to even one person in this world and if it helps just *one person find his or her soulmate*, the effort would have been worth it. The key to reading this book is to try out what it says. It has very simple messages to convey. You can start practising any of them right away and I would encourage you to do so. Take a leap of faith and just throw yourself into 'DOING' what this book says and you will be surprised by the results. If you are trying to get married and you really follow what this book says, I can assure you there is a 99.99 per cent chance you will find your life-partner in the next nine weeks!

So go ahead and start on your exciting journey and remember that at least *I* will be hoping and praying you find your true life-partner at the earliest!

SECTION ONE

Week One

❄

Decide What You Want

Interestingly, this is one of the most difficult questions to answer. Usually, we are clearer about what we don't want. But, if we are able to decide on what we want, I can assure you, we will get it.

'I want to get married,' is a thought a lot of us carry around in our minds. It could also be, 'I want to meet someone', 'I want a partner', etc. The point is: how detailed and defined is this thought to ourselves?

Let me take a simple example.

'I want to eat.' Sure. The next question is, *what* do I want to eat? Let's, for a moment, assume I want to eat Chinese cuisine. The next question would be, from which restaurant? I would then visualise or think about a restaurant and, depending on my storehouse of memories, associated thoughts and recommendations of friends or food reviewers, take a decision. Then, I would go to the particular restaurant and order the desired meal.

What I am saying is that we need to think of the *specifics* in order to convert a thought or desire into reality. Just thinking that I want to eat will not make Chinese food automatically arrive in my mouth.

Surprisingly, when it comes to things like wishing to get married, we often leave our thoughts at that vague level of, 'I want to get married'. Following that desire, we do start to act on it in terms of meeting people or getting on to online wedding sites, but what we do not realise is that before doing all this, we need to be more specific in terms of thought.

So the task for the first week is to **decide what you want**. Some of you reading this book may already have a list of what you want. Kudos to that! You even may be carrying it around and reading it over and over again, morning, noon and night. If you are doing so, you will find your partner very soon.

In case you are not doing so, let's examine how to go about it. Remember, it is extremely important to have fun and enjoy the whole process. To decide what we want, we need to clearly put down the following thoughts on paper, mobile phones, iPhones, iPads or whatever else you are comfortable with. What we put down is what we want and it could look something like this:

I want to get married by......(a date which is nine weeks from now) *to the woman/man of my dreams who has the following qualities:*

1. Is intelligent and has a great sense of humour.
2. Is caring.
3. Is tall and good-looking.
4. Belongs to my community.
5. Is well-educated and well-placed in society.
6. Dresses well and has a great sense of hygiene.
7. Knows how to dance...or sing....

Once you have this list ready, go over it again. The first thing to check is the number of points on it. I have found that, ideally, the list could have anywhere between four to ten items. This is not to say we cannot have less than four or more than ten. However, somewhere between four to ten points allows us to be more specific.

The next step is to analyse the list. I am assuming you have put down your own list by now. In case you have not, I strongly urge you first do this exercise with your own list.

First, examine the points mentioned on the list and do a forced ranking on the same. This means, rate them in order of priority, with the most important one on top and so on. For example, depending on your individual preference or priority, your list may look something like this.

1. Is tall and good-looking.
2. Is well-educated and well-placed in society.
3. Is intelligent and has a great sense of humour.
4. Belongs to my community. *(My experience is that people start by looking for a match from their own community, especially where parents are involved, and then graduate to outside their community, especially in India, a fact borne out of a matrimonial page in any newspaper where the listings by community far outnumber the general listings.)*
5. Knows how to dance.
6. Is caring.
7. Dresses well and has a great sense of hygiene.

This step is necessary because it helps us prioritise things. Next is to make the list a little crisper, by removing 'Is' from our list, as shown below.

1. Tall and good-looking.
2. Well-educated and well-placed in society.
3. Intelligent and a great sense of humour.
4. From my community.
5. Can dance.
6. Caring.
7. Dresses well and has a great sense of hygiene.

Now that the list is tighter and more organised, you will need to pick out the three things that matter the most to you from it. Let's see how this works.

Choose the three non-negotiable attributes you desire in a partner. The list then might look something like this.

1. Tall and good-looking.
2. Intelligent and a great sense of humour.
3. From my community.

The logic for removing 'Well-educated and well-placed in society' is that if the person is tall, good-looking, beautiful and intelligent and moves in the circles that you move in, there is an implied probability that she or he will be well-educated and well-placed too. Agreed it may not always be the case, but the probability is high and being reasonably intelligent is in most cases a prerequisite for this point. In essence, if two of the shortlisted points are satisfied, there is a chance that this point will also come to pass.

Again, the reason for removing 'Caring' from the list is that if the person is really intelligent and has a sense of humour, then there is a good chance she or he may be caring. I believe that intelligence is a notch higher than just caring. A lot of guys/ girls are caring, but do not have the intelligence that would set them apart. However it is difficult to categorise, which is why I have said that this is a forced ranking.

I removed 'Dresses well and has a great sense of hygiene' from the list because I class this as a part of my own concept of good-looking. I do understand that being good-looking may have nothing to do with dressing well and personal hygiene. What I am trying to say here is that when I evaluate a potential partner and classify her as beautiful from my perspective, I would also in some way evaluate her on her sense of dressing and on her basic sense of hygiene.

I removed 'Can dance' because whilst that can be a nice criterion to have, I believe the other three are more important.

In a nutshell: if the first three points are not present, there is a likelihood that the others might not be there as well. Whereas, if the first three attributes are there, then there is a strong possibility the others will be there too.

The reason for this exercise is to narrow down the three main criteria which you believe are critical. This shortlist will help you make quick decisions and prevent you from wasting time in case they are not present.

Again, an important question here is, is this the right way? It could be possible that your soulmate may not have these particular attributes but may have other desirable qualities. Won't you be overlooking those if you just concentrate on these? Will you be missing out on someone?

My answer to this is in two parts:

1. The above exercise needs to be done in conjunction with another principle, 'Trust your instincts,' which will be explained in Chapter 3. It means that even if we meet a person who apparently has none of the listed qualities and yet we find ourselves attracted to her, we need to follow our instinct. This is why we need to treat the above listing process merely as a tool, which can help us.

At the same time, we cannot use the tool to the exclusion of our instincts.

2. You have to start somewhere. Listing out what you really want helps you in a scenario where your instincts are unable to guide you. For example, if looks are important to you, and you meet someone whose looks do not attract you in any way, then there really is no point in spending time with that person.

I need to make an important clarification here regarding what I mean by 'looks' since I can already sense that some of you are thinking, 'Looks are not everything!' Or, 'Does it mean that unless I am good-looking there is no hope for me?'

Good looks are relative. Everyone has their own idea of beauty, including you, and it is important that your criterion is met as, after all, you have to live with and thereby see that person for a very long time.

Coming back to the three points, let's see if we can put them together in one sentence.

I am so happy now that I have found this tall, good-looking, intelligent/ beautiful guy/ girl from my community who has a great sense of humour.

This is now the specific sentence that you can use.

Obviously, you will tailor-make a completely different sentence for yourself, and when you do, you will frame it with: 'I am so happy now...'

It is important we state it in this fashion in the present

tense to ensure that the person we are looking for actually manifests.

So what have you achieved?

Essentially, a specific sentence which encapsulates your specific desire. Now, read it over once. Read it again, slowly and carefully. As you do, you will see that, apart from being alert to the contents of this sentence, you will also be conscious of the criteria you have taken out. This is natural and it should be that way.

If at this point you feel like tweaking your statement a little, do it and then once it is final, memorise it. Given that you have been through so much of effort in writing it, it is already imprinted on your mind.

The key is to say it out loud and clear. As you read or go through the sentence in your mind, slow down and visualise each of the attributes. For example, how tall is tall for you? Imagine that height in a person, and in this manner, imagine a person with all the qualities you want.

Have this sentence ready in about three to four days. Focus on what you really want. Of course, there is always the possibility that your Prince/ Princess Charming might suddenly land up and sweeps you off your feet without this too. If that happens in the next one or two days, throw this book away and get on with life!

Now that you have your sentence, let it sink into your subconscious. Repeat it to yourself before you go to sleep and when you wake up in the morning. Infuse it with emotion and feel good about it. Imagine the person you are visualising in front of you as if he is there. Make this a habit.

If you do this faithfully and with conviction, you have really decided what you want. And once you decide what you want, it is only a matter of time before it manifests. This is simply what you need to do in the first week and this is the starting point for you in getting what you want, and in this context, a suitable life-partner or companion.

I remember having heard a saying: *The definition of insanity is doing the same thing over and over again and expecting different results.*

We have to change what we do, to get different results. Especially now that we have embarked on one of life's most important aspects, it is important we be open to change.

For some of you who are reading this book, you may already be engaged or are seeing someone. If you are sure about the person you are seeing, you don't really need to read this book. But, in case you are unsure about him or her, then do this exercise and discover what it is you are really looking for and whether or not your fiancé or boyfriend matches up to what you want.

It may sound tough. After all, we also battle with the saying, 'Love is blind' or 'Love is unconditional'. Therefore, it is important for us to be clear about what we want and, if necessary, revisit our written declaration and see whether it is really important to us.

For example, would you reject a guy who had all the

qualities you want but who was not tall enough for you? Does it really matter?

These are tough questions and the answers lie within you. It also calls for a certain amount of self-analysis which is beyond the scope of this book. However, I will leave you with an important tool for understanding this concept a little better.

Think about *why* you want the person to be tall. If it is something *you* want and it has emanated from *your own instinctive being,* then it is fine. However, if it is something you want because *others* have said it should be that way, then re-examine your thoughts.

The point is to rely on your own judgement and be happy with your own set of criteria. After all, each one of us is responsible for everything that happens to us.

Finally, be happy with what you have decided and take this moment to move on to the next chapter.

Week Two

Make That Move

Now that you are sure about what you want, it is time for you to take action.

Recently, I went for my six-year-old son's Sports Day in school. It was an extraordinarily well-arranged event, with a huge dragon, group karate shows, ball drills, etc. I was impressed with the show considering it was organised by Class 1 and Class 2 students.

After it was over and the parents were leaving, I had an urge to go up to the principal and compliment her on what a great show it was. She was surrounded by people, but I made my way to her and expressed my appreciation. She was visibly overjoyed. I realised I must have been one of the few people who had gone up to her for that purpose. And it made a difference to her. My wife later told me that the principal was really happy that someone had praised the event.

The question is: why didn't so many other parents do the same? Didn't they like the show? Did they not care?

They probably liked the event. They did care. But they just didn't rouse themselves up to actually go and express their feelings. And that's the fact of the matter – that *on countless occasions, we don't do what we think we should. And then the moment passes.*

There have been hundreds of times when I have hesitated. Yet, there have been times when I have taken action and the results have been amazing. Always.

What I am saying here is: 'Make that move'.

Has it ever happened to you that you see someone who you want to approach and express your appreciation for what he or she does, but you hesitate? And the more you doubt your move, the more difficult it becomes to convince yourself to go up to the person. Finally, the moment passes and the person walks away and your opportunity too goes with him or her.

A similar incident can happen with a potential life-partner. You may feel like going up and striking a conversation, but you hesitate and the opportunity is gone. (I am not talking here about some habitual conversation-makers who have a tendency to barge into a person's privacy. I know there are such cases, but let us not allow that to negate what I am saying about approaching someone.) I have done it and it's easy. Remember, if you talk to a person politely, in ninety-five per cent of the cases they will respond positively. That's what really matters.

So what I am saying here is, 'Make that move when you see a window of opportunity.' Don't let potential partners fade away just because you didn't have the courage to go up and make conversation.

This, however, is easier said than done. So how should you practise this? How do you make it a habit?

Start now. Start talking to strangers, start doing those impulsive things you feel like doing and start letting yourself go.

Before I elaborate on this, I need to make an important distinction here about what I mean by being impulsive. What I am saying is: 'Do impulsive things which make you happy, in the given context, but do *not harm* another person.' The following examples are some of the impulsive things that you can do which do not harm others.

- Talk to a stranger in the lift.
- Go out for lunch with the group instead of eating at office.
- Buy that expensive dress.
- Get yourself a foot massage and give the person a huge tip.
- Talk to the person sitting next to you on the flight.

The following examples are some impulsive things you should *not* do.

- Make fun of someone.
- Physically touch or assault a person.
- Tell someone that they are wrong.
- Abuse someone.

The philosophy is simple. You can do anything you choose to do as long as it does not harm someone else.

The important question is how to put this in action. It is easy to theorise about it, but actually doing it requires a mental shift. It implies working on your self-esteem, practising it and making it a habit. That's what I did as well.

Many years ago I was a very reserved person and just the thought of walking up to a stranger and starting a conversation seemed odd. It still does sometimes. Now I have trained myself to do it and it yields wonderful results.

You must be wondering how all this will help us.

In the first week you decided what you wanted. You now need to take inspired action to convert what you want into reality. When I say inspired action, I mean action that is different from forced action, which does not feel good.

To put it simply, if you have decided what you want from a life-partner and you see a potential candidate at the airport, what do you do?

What you need to do is to quickly take in the surroundings, assess the situation and approach the person and strike up a conversation with him or her. It's a judgement call. If it doesn't seem right, don't do it. But if it seems right and you feel yourself hesitating, wondering what the person will think, what others will think, etc, then just push yourself and go ahead. That is what I mean by 'Make that move.'

The above is a very simple example. There are many other things you can do in terms of making your move. One simple step is to register on some online sites that assist you in searching for a life-partner. Many have already done that.

The biggest hurdle you will have to overcome is the concern about what others will think. Believe me, other people are generally not thinking about you at all – they are too busy thinking about themselves. So go ahead and make that move and it will take you on an amazing journey.

What I am suggesting here is one of the easy ways to start changing oneself. This is one of the purposes of this book and hence if you really want to do this, try and follow the suggestion given below meticulously for a week.

Start talking to everyone you meet in your daily life, people you do not normally acknowledge beyond a normal courtesy. I am talking about the pantry boy, the guard, your office receptionist, kabariwala, milkman, newspaper guy, driver or even the waiter serving you at a restaurant.

If you think about it, do we ever ask the name of a waiter in a restaurant and make any effort to talk to him? Do we talk to the guard below our building and ask him about his family? I am sure some of us do. At the same time, given our hectic schedules and our natural tendency to remain within our comfort zone, stop us often from making the effort.

If you are sitting in a public place, try and talk to someone next to you. Just do it and see what happens.

The first time you speak to someone whom you normally would not, it might feel awkward, but it will definitely be a start to overcoming the barrier within you. Approach and talk to at least three people a day for a week, and you will have done it twenty-one times in one week. That is the time frame needed to transform an act into a habit. You will see how much people appreciate your gesture of talking to them and asking after them.

Apart from talking, listen to people. Try to get out of your own world for a moment and look at things from their perspective. Very soon you will realise it is actually fun to talk to people.

How does all this help? It helps us take definitive and inspired action. It may be in the form of speaking to a stranger. It may also be in the form of professing your love for your companion who may be dilly-dallying about it. It all boils down to the fact that we have to *do* things rather than just *think* about them.

I'll let you in on a secret. Generally people love being talked to. We are social animals and it is in our nature to communicate with people around us. We are constantly seeking love and appreciation. It is a need deeper than hunger, deeper than any other desire we have. Yet we often ignore this need.

We go through life glued to our cell phones or iPads, chatting to people and friends who are far away while ignoring the people around us.

So, assuming you have followed what we have been

talking about and you have decided to do what I suggested, start doing it and see how it feels.

When someone wants to get married or engaged, he obviously approaches the matter with some sort of strategy. In India, youngsters may leave it to their parents. (Though nowadays, even if parents find a possible partner, it is finally the youngsters' choice to go ahead or not.) Some might look for a partner themselves, meeting and dating peers, looking for that relationship which might culminate in marriage.

All of the above require action. Sometimes, we may find things happening accidentally to someone. On the face of it, some people seem lucky. They find their soulmates apparently without any effort, whereas some never seem to click with the right person.

In reality, it is not about luck, but about intention. That is why I mentioned in the very first chapter that we need to be clear about what we want. Remember, the people who seem lucky are probably the most clear in their head about what they want. In fact, they are so clear that their clarity manifests into reality for them.

To reiterate, you first need to be sure of what you want and then take whatever action you can to make that a reality.

So just go out there and take action!

I would also like to assure every reader that if you scrupulously follow this chapter and actually do as I have said for a week, it will not only help you find your true soulmate but it will also alter the way you experience life. Trust me on this and just try it.

I will give you a personal example of how mental clarity combined with definitive action set the course of my life.

As a confused youngster, I enrolled for a degree in architecture. While studying the subject, I realised I was not cut out for the hours of drafting this profession required. I felt that I could never work in an architect's office and would be better off in the organised corporate sector. I wanted this for two reasons: I knew my skills lay in marketing, business development and managing people. I also knew that these corporate entities paid substantially better than architectural firms.

Though I did not know it then, it was the 'deciding-what-you-want phase' for me. The only thing I did was talk passionately and think endlessly about my dream job.

One day, my wife-to-be, who also studied with me, pointed out an advertisement in the newspaper which asked for architects who could sell glass.

I took action; I applied. I flew down to Mumbai and attended the interview where I was asked the question, 'Why would an architect want to sell glass?' I answered that if a computer science engineer could sell computers, then why couldn't an architect sell an architectural product?

I got the job. All my subsequent career moves emanated from there. The point is, it all happened because I was clear about what I wanted and I took action.

I would like to add a word of caution here, especially when we are talking about a man-woman relationship. Making a move does not include grabbing an unwilling lady and giving her a hug or a kiss.

Yes, there will be occasions when you will not be sure of what to do but that's where you need to use your judgement. For people who need to understand more about this, I would suggest you read some excellent books that are available in the market that give tips on how to interpret body language, how to understand the opposite sex better, etc. These will provide you with excellent tools and strategies. However, at the end of the day, it is you who will have to make the choice and hence the move.

In man-woman relationships, especially where you are evaluating each other as potential partners, it can sometimes put you under stress. This is more so in cases where you have just met, either through your parents or maybe through the Internet. It may be your first or second meeting and you are desperately trying to gauge what the other person is like, whether he or she likes you, whether he or she will be the right choice, etc. Often, these meetings are stressful and in a way counterproductive.

In a country like India, sometimes, it's not socially appropriate to meet a prospective partner more than two or three times to make up one's mind, though this scenario is gradually changing.

I agree it's a tough call. After all, there is no guarantee that if you meet a person ten times, it will definitely work out with that person. In fact, it could work the other way round – the more you meet a person, the less you might want to jump into marriage with him or her.

So how do we overcome all this? That's where our next chapter, 'Trust Your Instinct', comes into play.

Week Three

✻

Trust Your Instinct

Now that you have decided what you want and have started taking action, you need to learn how to trust your instincts.

An instinct may be defined as:

- An inborn pattern of behaviour that is characteristic of a species and is often a response to specific environmental stimuli.
- A powerful motivation or impulse.
- An innate capability or aptitude: for example 'an instinct for tact and diplomacy'.

Sometimes, we are intuitively attracted or repulsed by a person without any rational reason. Our subconscious takes over and sends our conscious mind that clear message.

That's what is instinctual knowledge. We all have it. The question is: do we follow our instinct? Do we trust it?

It's a difficult question to answer.

Sometimes, despite our instincts telling us one thing, we are unable to follow them because the logical side of our brain tells us that it is not viable from a social or work-related point of view. Thus, we override our gut reaction for the sake of being fair and unbiased.

However, when it really matters to us, I sincerely believe we should trust our instincts. Experts believe in the power of the subconscious mind to send us signals about a situation or person far before our rational mind can comprehend the same. I have often trusted my instincts and have found that it has served me well. There was a time when I used to be involved in theatre. In plays that had large casts and a huge number of people to be auditioned, we would have just about ten minutes to select an actor. Theatre groups require people to get along with each other. Long rehearsals and constant practise sessions are fertile grounds for dissent and conflict which have an adverse effects on the performance. Therefore, when choosing people, apart from their acting skills, we also had to evaluate them on their ability to interact with others.

So how did we do this in ten minutes? We used our instincts. Were we being fair? Again – a tough question.

Especially if we were rejecting a good actor just because we felt he or she would not gel with the group. At the end of the day, it's a choice we need to make and depending on that choice we pay the price of the outcome.

I only deviated once from using my instincts and I happened to take into the group a person who had been recommended by someone I could not refuse. I paid the price for that.

I am, therefore, convinced that in matters such as choosing a life-partner, our instincts are important. We need to trust them.

If your instincts warn you against a potential partner, follow them and steer clear of the person. Do not fall into the trap of giving another try to someone who instinctively repels you. You are wasting your time.

Is it being too presumptuous? Maybe yes. But, if you go back and analyse your first impressions, you will mostly find them to be correct.

On the positive side, and this is where it really works, there are some people whom you instinctively seem to like. Spend more time with them.

In these cases, make allowances for the person not being exactly as tall, beautiful, a great dancer or any other external attribute you want, as you would want him or her to be. If you like the person and your instincts draw you towards him, then give him a chance. The likelihood of things turning out well will be higher.

Assuming you agree with the above, one of the most

difficult things is to recognise when your instincts are telling you something about a person. How do you decode them to let you know in clear terms whether to proceed not? This is also complicated by the fact you may be operating under a powerful sense of physical attraction which may seem to override other considerations.

Following and trusting your instincts requires a little bit of practise. One of the easiest ways to let our subconscious take over is to relax. We are often so stressed about things that we are oblivious to our instincts. To illustrate this point, let me take you through a typical meeting between two potential life-partners.

The man – let us name him Ajay for the time being. The woman – let us name her Rashmi. The action between them is set in Mumbai.

Ajay is supposed to meet Rashmi on a Friday evening at 6 pm after office. This is their first meeting and they have decided on the coffee shop at Hotel Taj Land's End as the venue.

He is excited about this meeting. He liked Rashmi's photographs on the Internet and enjoyed talking to her over the phone. He appreciated the fact that she came across as friendly without going overboard. He wonders how she will be in person and whether they will click.

He is worried about two things. One is his hair which has started to thin. He is acutely conscious of his receding hairline and though he knows he has decent looks, he feels that girls prefer men with a thick head of hair.

The other thing bothering him is whether he should suggest a drive or a movie after coffee? Or would that be too forward for the first meeting? He really can't figure out what to do and ultimately decides to leave it for the moment.

Rashmi, on the other hand, is in a tizzy. She has to finish office, go home, change, get dressed and then come all the way back to Taj Land's End. She is getting a little tired of doing this and is wondering how this guy will turn out.

Thankfully, with all the rushing around, she does not have the time to worry too much about him. He sounded okay over the phone and seemed to have a sense of humour. He also looked quite impressive in the photograph he sent.

She only wishes she were fairer.

At 6 pm, by the time they manage to reach Taj Land's End, they are both a bit on edge. Anticipation mounts for Rashmi as she enters the hotel lobby and scans it for Ajay.

She sees him and says, 'Hi.' He reciprocates with a suggestion that they go to the coffee shop. They are talking easily and, despite herself, Rashmi finds herself evaluating his height, his hair and his overall bearing. Somehow he had seemed much bigger in his photograph, whereas he is actually quite slender.

Ajay, on the other hand, is thinking that she had seemed fairer in her photograph, but she has a nice smile.

They order some snacks and talk about various things – their interests, careers, hobbies, movies they like, future plans, etc. It is difficult to explain to a new person, in so short a time, one's life-trajectory thus far, the important conclusions and understandings that have been arrived at. But they are trying to do so.

Ajay explains how it is key for him that the woman he marries is modern yet traditional, someone willing to compromise.

Rashmi takes a strong stance as far as any compromise is concerned and asks him what he means by it. He is unable to give her a satisfactory answer and for a while there is silence.

Then they move on to a different topic; she asks him about his future plans. He says he is considering overseas career options.

They talk about work and she senses he is a cribber. She starts losing interest. He reads her mind and suddenly wants to set things right. With an air of bravado, he asks her if she would like to go for a drive.

He likes her and feels the need to push their interaction forward.

She, on the other hand, needs some space before she makes her next move. So, instead of a drive, she suggests they take a walk along Bandstand.

As they walk, she begins to feel better. They make general conversation and then decide to call it a day after agreeing to meet again.

There is a chance, if you are reading this, that you might have been through a somewhat similar experience.

If you have, you will realise that what I have captured here is only a fraction of what goes on in people's minds in such interactions. Hundreds of thoughts crowd our minds and one tries to make sense of them all at once. One tries to evaluate and impress the person at the same time.

It, therefore, goes without saying that the above situation is stressful. The stress of such a situation makes you incapable of listening to, or even understanding, your instincts. So how do you ensure a calm state of mind that will allow you to be mindful of your instincts?

There are a few ways to achieve this.

The most effective way is to learn to relax in situations like these. This allows your natural instincts to take over. There are other ways as well which include attending training sessions on communication, body language, team building, etc. There are books which guide you to handle these situations and one can refer to them as well.

Since the purpose of this book is to recommend a simple way to learn to trust our instincts, I will focus on the first point, i e, how we can try to relax in situations like this.

Though it may sound difficult at first, it is essentially a case of how you orient your thinking. On a personal level, I have always experienced greater success with people and situations when I am relaxed. At the same time, a certain amount of nervous tension is also good for us. In fact, slightly increased adrenalin levels are equally important to be able to take those impulsive decisions.

So how do we ensure a balance between being suitably charged up for the encounter and relaxed at the same time?

This can be done in two ways:

1. Let yourself go with the flow. Have faith in a positive outcome.
2. Focus only on the exciting possibilities of the encounter. Fantasise if required.

There are a total of four sentences in the two ways mentioned above. The rest of this section will elaborate on the meaning of these four sentences. Read them carefully if you believe this will help. They have helped me in innumerable situations, including in writing this book.

'Let yourself go with the flow.'
What this means is that we need to let go of our desperate need to control every possible situation. For example, while I can control my actions of reaching a place on time, I cannot control whether or not the other person reaches there on time. I can keep a reasonable margin to ensure that I reach on time, however I cannot control situations like a major traffic jam which eats away into that margin. So, do not try to control things over which you have no control.

In a social encounter, we can control our behaviour — we can be polite, kind, generous, but we cannot control the other person's behaviour.

Nothing, and I repeat nothing on earth, can force a person to like another person. It just happens. In the broad scheme of things, if we are destined to have a particular person as a life-partner, we will have that person. If we are not, then we will not. However, this does not mean that we do not take action. Our destiny depends on the actions we take and we cannot fulfil it by the total lack of action. So the best way to counter all this is to relax and go with the flow.

Don't get hung up on trying to be perfect. Be yourself, be relaxed and be observant. Not only will it help you better evaluate a person, but you will also come across as genuine and grounded. We often try to be someone we are not, primarily in order to live up to a self-mage thrust upon us by society.

Personally speaking, I am clumsy by nature. I tend to trip over things. I lack the refined social graces of fine dining or high-end table manners acceptable in society. While I am able to chew my food with my mouth closed, I am not really a graceful social eater and I sometimes tend to stuff slightly large helpings into my mouth. And by God…I so enjoy it!

Has the above affected my relationships or my marriage? No, it has not. Sure, most people I meet notice my lack of grace, but it has not affected any of my relationships.

Don't succumb to the need to live up to someone else's image of ourselves. On the contrary, live up to the image of who you really are and who you want to be. The only rider on that is that none of your resultant actions should harm anybody.

Once you are comfortable with yourself, you will be able to go with the flow. And when you do that, you will suddenly find good things happening with you, which brings us to the next line:

'Have faith in a positive outcome.'
This means that if you expect a positive outcome you are likely to get one. This also draws on the famous, 'Law of Attraction', which essentially states that like attracts like. Hundreds of books have been written about the 'Law of Attraction', therefore I will not elaborate on it. What I will focus on here is a practical way to relax and have faith in a positive outcome.

The biggest hurdle to this principle is our self-doubt. One of the reasons we have self-doubt is our worry about the outcome and its import to us.

Let me give a small example of how you can identify this.

I care a lot about how silly I look when I try to dance. On the rare occasions when I try to dance, I worry about how odd I must look. With the result, I still can't dance. I have often thought about taking classes but never got around to doing so. Whenever someone says I should dance, I get up but become conscious and am unable to let go. On the few occasions that I have let go (probably after a few drinks!), I have apparently shaken a leg quite decently.

So this is one aspect I am still working on with the hope that, one day, I shall crack it.

I enjoy watching a good movie now and then, but don't like planning for the same. So I usually take a chance at getting a ticket. Interestingly enough, ninety-nine per cent of the times I get the desired ticket, quite effortlessly. It just happens. My wife and friends will vouch for it. Why does this happen?

I am convinced this happens because I am relaxed about it and certain that I will get what I want. In this regard, I do not have worries or self-doubt. I just expect it and it happens.

If you think about your life, you will also find such things happening with you – with things you want and with things which you are not unduly concerned about. Identify these things and you will find the key to expecting a positive outcome.

All this may sound simple or complicated depending on your frame of mind while reading this, but it is truly one of the most crucial steps in realising your dreams, which in this case is to find a suitable life-partner.

Spend a couple of days identifying a few things that come easily to you. Analyse the mind-set you have at that time. Try to replicate the same in your relationships/meetings with prospective partners. In a nutshell, 'Go with the flow and have faith in a positive outcome.'

The second point was:

'Focus only on the exciting possibilities of the encounter. Fantasise if required.'
This is another method that can help you be more relaxed about a situation. An encounter with anyone has exciting possibilities, ranging from acquiring an acquaintance to a lifelong friend or partner.

Whatever the outcome may be, the art is to imagine all the exciting possibilities of the encounter before you enter it. While everything you visualise may not turn out just so, the very process of it will relax you. Focusing on the exciting possibilities and even fantasising about them puts us in a positive frame of mind and gives us a rush of adrenalin that we need for the interaction.

For example, you could imagine going on a dinner date or watching a movie together, or how both of you will look during your wedding, where you would like to go for your honeymoon, and so on.

This is the opposite of worrying about how the interaction will turn out and what kind of an impression you will make. After all, tormenting yourself about things will not solve them. Taking positive action will.

To conclude, it is essential for you to trust your instincts if you are to find that perfect companion. One of the ways to do so is to practise relaxed interactions with people. Remember, you are now in your third week and apart from having decided what you want and having 'made that move', you have now learnt to relax and trust your instincts.

Since many of you might read this book in one continuous sitting, it is essential to be aware that you can start applying any of these steps immediately. There is nothing stopping you from applying them in your day-to-day lives as well!

We now move on to the next chapter which talks about 'learning to listen'.

Week Four

❖

Learn to Listen

D o you really listen to other people when they are talking
to you? If yes, great, and I suggest you skip this chapter.
If not, then you need to ask yourselves, why not?

I think one of the reasons for not listening to others is
that we are only too eager to have people listen to us. Even
when we do listen, we tend to have a parallel conversation
running in our mind about our next response.

Today's busy world and our penchant for multitasking
often take a toll on our listening habits. Under constant
pressure to take quick decisions in this fast-paced life of ours,
we have forgotten the art of patiently listening to others.

In a way, everything starts with listening. Even the mere

act of reading this line is a form of listening: listening to my thoughts through the medium of this book.

Listening is, thus, perhaps one of the easiest things you can do to achieve your objective of finding your true life-partner. Unfortunately, you will never find a class or a course which focuses exclusively on listening. For some reason, we think listening is easy and therefore something we don't really need to learn.

I have found out over the years that it is one of the most difficult things to do. I have also understood that I owe all that I have achieved in my life to listening as intently as I could to people around me.

The question again is: How can you hone your listening skills and how will it help you find your life-partner?

It is easier to answer the second question of *how it will help* and I will answer that first.

When you speak, you are constantly giving away clues about who you are, how you think and what you intend to be. I have found that by listening intently to a person for about an hour you can more or less make out what he thinks about most things. To a certain extent, you can make out how he will react in different situations and what his take on life is in general. (I am talking about normal people here and not about trained CIA agents who I am told can speak in a fashion or manner which hides their true intentions.)

I once overheard a fellow student in my engineering college state that there was no way he would ever allow his wife to have a career. After all, he said, what would people say? According to him, people would think he didn't have the capability to earn enough money and hence his wife was working.

I don't wish to pass judgement on that viewpoint. All I want to highlight is that his statement gives us *an idea about his thought process.* All of us have our reasons for our beliefs and there may be nothing right or wrong about them. The only thing here is if he continued to have such a conviction but married a woman who strongly believed she needed to work for personal reasons, there would be potential cause for conflict. Of course, it is not as if such conflict cannot be resolved. It can be. But you might not want to enter into such a conflict situation at all.

Listening carefully allows you to evaluate people's thoughts, views and opinions that define them.

What we now have to *really listen for is whether my fellow-student actually meant what he said, or whether he was repeating something he had just heard.*

If, after further conversation, it transpires that he is merely parroting a view he heard, it could be that he is not so rigid about his belief and can be made to see another viewpoint. However, if he truly lives by that belief, and is inflexible about it, then his prospective life-partner might want to evaluate its implications before proceeding to the next step.

The question is, how do you gauge whether he is really serious or not? You do this by asking a few simple open-ended questions and then *listening* intently to his answers. If you do this carefully, you will understand what a person is all about. It will help you evaluate whether or not you might get along as a couple.

Listening allows you to carefully weed out potentially incompatible partners, and that is just one of the benefits. There is a far greater benefit – it allows you to understand what a person is really saying, without judging, but with empathy and unconditional love.

I say this from experience and I have found that if you listen to a person genuinely, you will start connecting with her on a level you previously thought impossible. For when we listen with all our attention, people can sense it and it fosters an inexplicable bond which contributes significantly to a possible relationship.

We all want to be heard. We all want somebody to listen to us and, more importantly, listen without judging us. Listening well therefore endears you to a person and there is a greater likelihood of her liking or falling in love with you. At a deeper level, it allows you to understand her better and respond accordingly. As you hone your listening skills, you will reach a level where, apart from listening to the first-cut view of opinions, you will be able to understand where they are coming from, and if they are temporary influences, then allows you to maybe help her discover her own voice.

Simple Ways to Hone Our Listening Skills

The first step is to acknowledge that you are having a parallel conversation in your head while 'listening' to another person.

It will help you realise where you are at that present moment and course correct. It may be easy for some and challenging for others. Focus on what the person is saying and try to keep track of what is going on in your mind. Let me elaborate.

Often, when a person is narrating a tough experience he went through, your mind is co-relating it to all the tough times you have had. It triggers a sort of memory recall for us and, sometimes, instead of really listening to what the other person is saying, *we start unconsciously preparing to relate the story of our own tough time.* It is one of our most natural reactions – to start mirroring the conversation, which typically means that we have stopped listening and are busy rehearsing our response. If we stop for a moment and think about this, we will realise that if a person is telling us about her problems, then what she is really expecting from us is understanding and acknowledgement. At that point in time, she does not want to hear our story, as that does not help her situation.

If we notice this about ourselves we have achieved the first step. The next step is to act on this realisation.

Often it's common to assume we know what the other person is going to say. We also assume that we know why the person is saying that.

Both these assumptions interfere with our ability to really listen to people. Therefore, spend some time during this week to analyse your listening quotient. After a few days, you will be able to identify the aforementioned patterns. Once that is done, it's time to take the next step.

How can we become better listeners? I will outline a few easy points in no particular order, which, if followed faithfully, can transform us overnight into excellent listeners and in a way change our lives forever.

1. Develop a genuine interest in the person you are listening to.
2. Suspend all judgement when listening. I repeat, 'suspend all judgement.'
3. Empathise with what the person is saying.
4. Briefly touch upon your own experience only if appropriate and if it gives comfort to the other person.

There are a lot more things we can do to listen better. However, for the purpose of simplicity let's just concentrate on the four points mentioned above and especially on the first two.

Develop a genuine interest in the person you are listening to

I agree it's a difficult thing to do. However, at the end of the day, if you really want to listen to somebody, you have to develop a genuine interest in her or else you will always be listening superficially.

There are various ways to develop this habit.

The first is, each time you are about to listen to someone, imagine you are throwing a switch in your mind to shut out everything save the desire to listen to what the person is saying.

It is important at this stage to make proper eye contact with the person. You will be surprised at the number of people who do not make eye contact when listening to somebody.

Another way is to imagine that the person you are listening to is a celebrity on a talk show. When you watch a talk show, you listen with all your attention. Your mind automatically conditions you not to speak or interrupt since the other person cannot hear you. The point is that often we listen with bated breath to what celebrities have to say, to the exclusion of even our family members, because we have developed a genuine interest in them. Try to recreate that with the people around and you will see the immediate difference in your life.

Without digressing from the point of how listening will help us find a life-partner, I would like to state that listening to our family members would also do wonders to our existing relationships. Just try it and see. In fact, try this with each one of your immediate family members, friends and colleagues and you will see the difference.

Suspend all judgement when listening

One of the things we constantly do is pass judgement on others. It is in our nature to try to size up people based on their appearance, looks, behaviour and what they say. When we are judging people and trying to slot them into a particular category, we are not really listening to them.

Therefore, try not to think of anything else. Just concentrate on what the person is saying. Try to understand their innermost thoughts. Acknowledge what they are saying without adding your own thoughts. Remember, when we are talking, we want to be heard, appreciated and reassured. We want to be acknowledged for who we are. So why not do the same for another?

Again, it is important to be relaxed about this. We can't be listening well if we are trying too hard. When we are able to accept people as they are, we will also find greater peace within ourselves. After a time, this begins to show and people around will sense it. It will make them want to spend time with you.

A note of caution here: Listening carefully to everyone is different from being an agony aunt, and I leave it to you to use your discretion to avoid becoming one.

- Empathise with what the person is saying.
- Relate your own experience only if appropriate and if it gives comfort to the other person.

These two points are self-explanatory. Empathise with the person talking, and share your experiences on the topic under discussion only if it helps the person feel better. Use the 'Feel, Felt, Found' method to express empathy and make a constructive suggestion. 'I know how you feel, I felt the same way, till I found that...' It is important, however, to draw a line here and not start relating some long-winded personal experience and take over the conversation.

It becomes easier for us to empathise with someone when we have gone through the first two steps of developing a genuine interest in them and viewing them without judgement.

A person can sense when we genuinely and sincerely empathise with them. As human beings, we desperately yearn to be heard, understood and acknowledged. When we know we are being listened to unconditionally it instils within us a huge sense of wellbeing.

I read somewhere recently that in today's world the amount of information a person receives in one day is equivalent to the total information a person would have received in his or her *entire lifetime* about three hundred years ago!

It is no wonder then that we have less and less time to really listen to people. But, if we make the effort to develop this habit, not only will it help us find our life-partner, but it will also help us keep our life-partner.

If out of this whole book, you are able to only take away the learnings from this chapter and follow them diligently, there is a ninety per cent chance you will get your life-partner in the next five weeks. I can almost guarantee it!

I hope you are listening…!

Week Five

Start Smiling

For many years of my life, I was under the impression that when I smiled my nostrils kind of flared out and my nose looked a little flattened. I laboured under the impression that I looked nice only when I had a serious expression on my face. Some people did tell me that I should smile a lot more and that it made me look good, but it had no real impact on me.

I continued to go through life with a serious expression and, by virtue of the same, a serious life.

Then about six years ago, I had the good fortune of associating with a Dale Carnegie master trainer who changed my life. It happened quite simply over a period of about three to four months.

There were two significant turning points which still remain in my mind and which convinced me of the power of smiling.

Since I had done some amount of public speaking, I had developed an ability to get up in front of an audience and turn on an imaginary switch within myself which transformed my personality. I became more vibrant and aware and it showed. At the same time, I smiled a lot when I was doing this. However, once I was off the stage, I would revert to my normal laid-back self and exude a general nonchalance that I erroneously thought suited me.

It was at one of these sessions that the master trainer noticed this and casually remarked that he would like to see more of my 'dynamic persona' offstage, and specially when I was sitting. He asked me to appear more interested and alert when at rest and also to work on smiling more often.

I followed his advice. I began sitting straighter and showing a genuine interest in things. More importantly, I became deliberate about smiling.

That was the first turning point.

The second turning point came a few months later when I was training a group of people in Hyderabad. By then, I was smiling a lot more and, by virtue of the same, appeared relaxed and approachable.

The six days' session in Hyderabad turned out to be a remarkable episode of my life. From a professional perspective, I achieved a 'hundred per cent exceed expectations' score from my trainees, which in hindsight was a significant achievement. However, what really made a difference to me was the reaction of the people I was training. Within a few days, I had established a special bond with some of them. I learnt that because of my open smile, I came across as a person who could be trusted, was approachable and in whom people could confide. It made me realise the huge impact that smiling had on our lives.

While smiling in itself may sound easy, it is actually not. Let's put this to the test. For one day, observe the expressions of the people around you. You will be surprised at the number of serious and tired faces you will see. Here, I am talking about observations made on a regular day, not when a person has just walked out after watching a comic film.

Keep looking at people and you will notice that sometimes they don't smile for hours on end.

Am I saying we should smile for no reason whatsoever? Smile incessantly, and have people believe we are crazy?

Yes. That's exactly what I'm talking about! Just try it for fun and see the difference. Start right now.

Force yourself to smile and keep doing so for at least thirty seconds. Soon, you will find your fake grin turning into a genuine one!

If you could see yourself in a mirror now, I can guarantee you look much better. Notice how we are all drawn to people who smile. Notice how a smile lights up someone's face. See how a person's eyes become brighter when they smile. Make it a practise to smile irrespective of the time and just keep doing it. (I assume we are mature enough not to smile when the situation is genuinely grim. But those moments are very few in our entire lives.)

It is important to dwell briefly on a concept here which talks about cause and effect. For example, we normally smile when we are happy. Therefore, happiness is the cause and smile the effect. A new theory suggests that if we imitate the effect we can sometimes manifest the cause. Simply put, it means that if we can force ourselves to smile we can in due course begin to feel happy.

The issue here is how does this help us find a life-partner?

We always react positively to a smile. We are instinctively drawn towards smiles whether we know it or not. It is a natural human reaction. Therefore, when we are interacting with possible life-partners they will simply be more attracted to us if we smile. It also increases our chances of being noticed and of people coming up and talking to us.

You must be wondering if all one has to do is smile to get a life-partner, then why aren't all doing so? In fact, I can sense your scepticism even as I write this. I completely understand the feeling as I have been through it myself. I must admit it took me a couple of years to understand the concept of 'smiling' myself and I hope you assimilate and practise it sooner than I did.

1. *Smile in all situations*. Usually we smile in response to something.
2. *We can attract people by having a smiling countenance*. Unfortunately, very few of us are able to smile for five

per cent of the day. Most of us do not even smile for two per cent of the day which is about twenty-nine minutes or *half an hour!* A great example of a person who has a wonderful smiling face that makes us watch him over and over again is Harsha Bhogle, the cricket commentator. Next time you watch him, see how he has a great smile on his face when he speaks.

3. *Fake it till you make it.* The key is to force yourself to smile till it becomes a habit. For one week just focus on smiling. Just keep saying to yourself, 'smile', 'smile', 'smile', 'smile', 'smile', 'smile', 'smile', 'smile', 'smile', 'smile', 'smile', 'smile', 'smile', 'smile'....

Smile at people around you and see the difference.

4. *A smile makes you more attractive to people.* It makes you communicate favourably with them. If you smile at them, they respond similarly. In short, the positive energy of smiling spirals up as we go through an interaction.

I once tried this advice at a job interview. Apart from drawing on my listening skills I also tried keeping a slight and attentive smile on my face for most of the part. It worked with amazing results. Though I did not finally go for that particular job, the feedback I got through the placement consultant was that the interview had gone fabulously and the person who had taken the interview was really impressed. When I thought over what I had done differently, I realised I had smiled a lot more than I usually do. This convinced me of the power of smiling. It made me realise that it works and since then I have constantly been trying to practise smiling.

The next time you travel through an airport take some time to notice people's expressions when they check in. You will see that more than ninety per cent of them will have very serious expressions. Just try being different for once and when your turn comes at the check-in counter, give a big smile to the lady or gent who is sitting behind it. See how it feels both for you and the other person. Once you do it you will realise what I mean. The point is, DO IT!

Use this week or rather set aside one week of your lives to practise smiling. Try it and see. It will become a lifelong habit which will help you not only in finding a partner but also in keeping your partner. Interestingly, it is a fact that in call centres, people are taught how to smile while speaking with customers since it is a proven fact that when we smile and speak, people can actually sense the smile in our voices.

Smile and reap its rewards.

Week Six

Visualise

The first principle in the mission of finding a life-partner is to have a clear vision of the desired qualities in him or her and then to encapsulate them in a sentence. Visualisation is a follow-on to that.

There are two parts to this.

1. Be convinced that visualisation can really help.
2. How to apply it so as to get results.

If we examine what we do every day, we will see that we involuntarily visualise many things, consciously or subconsciously, before actually doing them. For example, every day, I visualise awaking in the morning, making myself a cup of tea and sitting down to a relaxed reading session. It is an involuntarily visualisation but it impels me to the desired action. Visualisation is about:

- Imagining in great detail about where you want to be.
- Seeing in your mind's eye the end result that you want.
- Feeling the emotions that go with your having achieved what you wanted.
- Believing that you have already received what you wanted.

In a nutshell, visualisation is thinking about what you want to do before actually doing it.

To attract a life-partner, you have to first visualise the ideal person coming into your life to the extent that the desire actually manifests itself.

The question is, is it so easy that simply by thinking of something and visualising it, it will appear in our lives?

The simple answer is, yes, if you do it with passion and conviction, it will bring to you the perfect person you've been looking for.

Every great achievement we see around us is a result of visualisation. Of late, there are innumerable books and articles on the power of visualisation. If you are on the Internet and if you Google the word 'visualisation', you will find thousands of articles on the topic and you can be rest assured that it must be working for at least some people. By the same token, if it works for some people, it will work for you as well.

Visualisation is a tool to prime our subconscious mind which in turn guides us to what we actually want. It creates situations which will help you place yourselves in a better position to find a life-partner. It will help you focus on what you want to do which, in this case, is to find true love.

Many great athletes and sportsmen visualise their games before they go out to play as mental preparation to give it their best. They visualise their success before it happens.

It is imperative to understand one critical issue in the visualisation process and that is, always visualise what you want to achieve, not what you want to avoid.

We have a tendency to imagine and focus on that which we don't want. It's natural human behaviour to imagine the worst. However, we need to be very alert to this propensity and steer clear of it by instantly changing our mental patterns from negative to positive, from what we don't want to what we want.

Negative visualisation is a result of the fear psychosis created by what we see and hear in the news around us. By focusing on negative incidents, there is a real possibility of attracting them to us. Practise visualisation exercises which are positive in nature and which are also fun. Imagine different scenarios which are related to what you want and each of them has a great chance of materialising depending on the intensity of your visualisation. The more vivid and lifelike you can make your visualisation, the more effective it will be.

I have experienced it myself and can vouch for the power of visualisation by the very fact that you are reading this book. If I had not visualised it first, there is no way I could have sat down and written it in the manner that I have.

Another great advantage of visualisation is that it is an entirely private affair. It is something you can do in the privacy of your mind, anytime and anywhere.

When it comes to finding a life-partner through visualisation, there are innumerable things you can visualise. You can visualise how you might meet a potential life-partner, the scene of meeting her for the first time, how your future interactions will progress and the intimate romantic scenes that you want to experience. There are no restrictions on visualising about something which gives us joy and which is not harmful to us or anybody else.

Visualisation requires discipline, awareness and persistence for it to have effect. Most of us have a tendency to stay with a thought for a couple of minutes after which we tend to move on to other thoughts. Then, suddenly, we remember the visualisation exercise, go back to it, and after a minute again, we are distracted by other thoughts. A few such sessions do not really have the potential to yield a result and we lose our belief in the power of visualisation.

It is, therefore, important for us to spend some time on understanding how exactly to harness the power of visualisation so that we can use it effectively to help us find our life-partner.

Visualisation is a kind of meditation and it requires

concentration. Switch off all other distractions and focus on the exercise. Over a period of time, you will be able to develop an ability to recall your visualisations effortlessly. This happens when you visualise faithfully and emotionally. It is important to remember that if you want your visualisation to be effective, you must keep aside some time for it every day, even if it is five to ten minutes a day.

For some, it may help to write down what they want to visualise in order to crystallise their thoughts.

Let us take an example of how we can use visualisation to create a desirable scenario for a date with a prospective partner. 'Rashmi', who for the purpose of our exercise will be the visualiser, is to meet Vijay with whom she has fixed up a date for the next day at eight o'clock at a restaurant named Eat Around the Corner. They connected over a matrimonial website. They have never met, only exchanged notes over the phone. She sits on her bed, eyes closed. First and foremost, she recalls Vijay's voice on the phone. She remembers its attractively deep tone and smiles. Next, she imagines each step she will take in preparation for the meeting. Here's her thought process in her words:

"For once, I am ready early and I still have fifteen minutes to walk down to the restaurant, which, thankfully, is close-by. I am wearing a dark-blue blouse over beige trousers and I know I am looking good. This top makes me look very feminine. I have worn my favourite perfume, and my sandals and bag are perfectly coordinated. I take a last look at myself in the mirror and am happy with what I see! I wonder how

Vijay will be turned out and how he looks in real life. He looked attractive in the photograph he sent and I know he will live up to that image.

Finally, I am ready to step out of the house, I double-check to see if I have my house keys, and am off to Eat Around the Corner.

As I near the restaurant, I see a tall, impressive-looking guy standing at the entrance, talking on the phone. He is gazing straight ahead and I get a good look at him. Yes, it is definitely Vijay and, from what I see, he looks very handsome to me. He is tall with a thick head of hair and is wearing a light-blue, striped shirt and a pair of black jeans. His sleeves are rolled up and I can see his muscular forearms. As I step closer, I hear him say goodbye to someone and then he turns towards me. We recognise each other at almost the same instant. There is something about him which immediately appeals to me. I get the impression that he likes me too.

'I am on time,' he says smiling, 'and so are you.'

We shake hands and walk to the restaurant. Vijay holds the door open for me to enter first. There is something definitely charming about old-world courtesy! I feel happy and excited. Our first encounter, the most difficult and the most defining moment of all, has gone well. In fact, it has gone amazingly well compared to all the others I have had!

We sit at a table of our choice and the first thing he asks me is what is it I'd like to have. I decide on a coffee. He places our order and we start talking. Maybe it's his perfectly formed teeth, or the endearing dimple on his right cheek which flashes when he does so, but I like the way he smiles. There's a relaxed air about him and I get the feeling he is enjoying himself. For a moment, I feel that familiar twinge of apprehension as to whether he likes what he sees or not and then somehow it is gone.

I relax and plunge wholeheartedly into the joy of a light-hearted conversation. We discuss common likes and dislikes and discover that we both like Hollywood films, Indian classical music, reading and share an interest in cooking. He is also a stamp collector and he likes trekking.

I can sense he respects women. From our chat, I find that he is doing well in his job, that his family is in Delhi and that he has an older sister who is married and settled in London.

I am talking about myself, and I see him listening with genuine interest. We have a second round of coffee and before we realise it, it is half past nine!

Vijay politely suggests dinner and I jump at the offer. The evening ends at about eleven o'clock after a wonderful dinner at Out of the Blue and when he drops me off in front of my place I think I couldn't have asked for a more wonderful evening!

Without being overt, he suggests we meet again and promises to give me a call the day after and from the way he says it I believe him. I can sense a possible relationship happening here and something tells me he is most probably the man I have been looking for."

(Rashmi's visualisation ends here.)

That's one example of how we can visualise a date which is the first stepping stone towards starting a possible relationship. As will be evident, there are various other things people can imagine and it is natural that each person will visualise from their perspective.

Some of us may find this somewhat simplistic. It may also sound like we are trying to build up a kind of romantic make-believe world which is different from what really happens. I can almost hear ourselves saying, 'We need to be practical.'

My take on this is simple. If we believe the world around us is fraught with practical difficulties, then that is what we will experience. It is really a matter of what we believe. We see and experience whatever we want to. If we truly believe in the goodness and benevolence of the universe, then that is what we will experience. I have experienced it myself and hence can vouch for it. Therefore, my request to you is simple. Expect great things in life and there is an overwhelming possibility that you shall get them.

Visualisation is the planning, imagining and crafting of such great expectations.

When we are looking for a life-partner, this particular activity of visualisation is an extremely powerful tool. I had used it unknowingly throughout my teenage years and I met and married the most amazing woman I have known because I had always visualised knowing and being with a person like her. We have been together for over twenty years now and we still look forward to the simple joys of life like going out for a movie, having a nice dinner somewhere, or going for a walk in the evenings. It happened because that is the way I had visualised my relationship and I actually believed in it.

It's important to add here that it was only later that I realised I had been using the visualising technique unconsciously. At the same time once I realised the power of deliberate visualisation I have realised that it is possible to develop and get results with this process within a period of one week. Once I discovered that, I have used it on numerous occasions to manifest what I have visualised.

Visualisation is a tool that may be used at any time and at various phases of your search for a life-partner. You may already be in a relationship and maybe you need to pop the question of marriage. Maybe you are ready to get married but there is something that is bothering you and you need clarity. Maybe some difficult questions need to be asked and some tough decisions taken. For all these encounters it is beneficial to use the process of visualisation. Remember that while visualising you see a POSITIVE outcome for yourself. It has to be an outcome that you want. An outcome you would like to have.

Will this process always be successful?

From a philosophical perspective, it will always be successful if done properly. That is if done with proper conviction, faith and passion then things will materialise in more or less the same way that you had visualised it. However, since we are unable to always do it the way we are supposed to, there will be some times when what you visualise does not come to pass. What should you do then?

My answer is that you should keep your belief and keep trying. As you do that, you will become better at it and as you become better at visualising things the right way, you will see the scenes you visualised actually manifesting. Therefore, do not be disappointed if a few initial visualisations do not work. Keep trying and believe in yourself and you will suddenly find that things are working out exactly the way you want them to.

I know this may sound a little difficult and to some of us it may seem like a lot of hard work. At the same time, if we analyse it we will see that we would only want to visualise things that would give us joy. Therefore, spending time imagining things that give us joy cannot be too difficult a task. So go ahead and give yourself a shot at visualising the innumerable situations that could lead to your life-partner in the remaining three weeks!

Week Seven

Love Yourself

I mentioned in the last chapter that, in my personal opinion, the world gives us unlimited opportunities to work towards having a joyful life At the same time, it also creates situations which we take at face value and accept as our reality. What I am talking about here is the all-pervading sense of competition that this modern world has managed to create for us, wherein it seems that we always need to prove ourselves in some manner or the other.

Over the last few decades, a sense of competition has invaded almost every aspect of our lives and we seem to be left with very little choice but to compare ourselves to other people. It has created a situation whereby we tend to become self-critical. Every advertisement we see questions our beliefs and urges us to be better than what we are. Our jobs or our businesses, which are one of our most important sources of survival, promote the concept of 'ratings' which inevitably leads us to assess ourselves with a critical eye.

We seem to have agreed that there is something wrong with us and that we should be doing something to improve ourselves. We have reached a stage where we have accepted the anomaly of 'constructive criticism' wherein we are encouraged to take criticism positively.

What we need to understand is that just the way there cannot be 'constructive murder' or 'constructive assault', there can be no 'constructive criticism'.

We need to understand that no one, I repeat no one, and least of all ourselves, have the right to criticise ourselves. The reason for this is simple. Criticising ourselves means 'not loving ourselves' and I believe we need to learn how to 'love ourselves'!

Loving ourselves the way we are is the most important step in the quest for a life-partner. Unless you really and truly love yourself, why would anyone else love you? When you look at yourself, you wonder how you could be a bit better in some aspect or the other. We have lost the ability to love ourselves unconditionally. We are looking for reasons to love ourselves when the reason is staring us in the face. We have the right to love ourselves for exactly what we are right now, right here, no questions asked.

It is one of the greatest realisations I have had over the last few years and is an important component of helping you find the perfect life-partner.

Set this week aside to shower yourself with love! Look at yourself in the mirror and tell yourself, 'I love you'. It may sound silly at first but do it. See how it feels. If you have read about this or done this before it may be easier. If this is the first time you are hearing about this concept then let me elaborate on this a little further.

We are used to being self-deprecating. 'I am not good at this', 'I don't think I can do this', 'I am not one of those intelligent ones', 'I am obviously not as good-looking as Katrina', 'I am beginning to feel old', and the list goes on.

It's a never-ending list which we seem to accept as part of our lives. We have fallen into an involuntary mode of comparing ourselves to others around us which leads to two sorts of reactions. We either feel a fleeting sense of glee when we realise we are better off than someone else, or a despairing emptiness when we think someone else is far better off than us. Neither of the above reactions is of any long-term use to us. They only remind us that we are not as good as we think we should be. Ultimately, there will always be someone or the other in our estimation who will seem to be better off than us. Therefore, unless we are able to stop comparing ourselves (and sometimes even our families) to others we will keep thinking that something is wrong with us.

In order for others to love us, it is important to love

ourselves first. The question is, how do we suddenly start loving ourselves?

For some of you this may be easy. Some might be thinking that they already love themselves enough, and some might already be practising this. However, I still recommend that all read the rest of this chapter for there are no limits to learning how to love ourselves more. It is a constantly evolving experience and we can never really love ourselves enough.

Some of us may have a tendency to confuse the above with self-obsession or self-indulgence. For example, I have often been asked the question that if a corrupt politician is hoarding away money for himself, isn't he actually 'loving' himself? Isn't he trying to obtain a greater level of happiness? The answer is an emphatic 'no' because there can be no love when we are *morally wrong*. The corrupt politician's actions are not actions of love but actions spurred on by a sense of insecurity and fear. These emotions are far removed from love and this is certainly not how we should love ourselves.

When we talk about love, we are talking about a deep, unconditional love for ourselves which when experienced properly allows us to develop a great sense of inner peace and happiness.

Now that we have discussed the pros and cons of loving ourselves it is important to see how we can practise them in a manner that is easy and simple. This may seem a little hard and funny in the beginning but eventually it can also be something that can be really enjoyed.

One of the easiest ways to start doing this is by pampering ourselves. While some of us may already be doing this, a lot of us hold back from the simple joys of life which we deserve. Yet if we analyse what is holding us back we will realise it is no one else but ourselves. So if eating a 'sizzling chocolate brownie' is what you like, go ahead and have it. If you feel like watching a movie, take half a day off from work and go for it! I know work is important and I don't deny that we need to be dedicated to it, but taking half a day off will not really change anything. If you have been thinking of splurging on that suit go ahead and do it.

Start by doing these simple things because these are easy and fun to do. After all, why would you choose to do them unless you really enjoy doing so.

Force yourself to indulge yourself for the first few days of the week. For some of us this may sound simple but I have often found that after the first couple of instances we seem to go back to our regular lives. So do it for a week.

One of the ways to generate self-love is by looking into the mirror, into your eyes and telling your reflection, 'I love you', many, many times. This may work for some and may not work for others. Few will find it difficult, funny or even embarrassing and it might take them some time and practise to come to terms with doing this regularly. Yet it is the most direct way to start the process which if pursued will prove very effective. For some lucky ones it will work instantly.

This method makes us realise that we are not used to taking time out to love ourselves. That will be apparent by the sense of strangeness we will feel when we first try this. At the same time, if we can keep at it we will realise that it is possible to love ourselves a lot more than we currently do.

Another method which works for me is to visualise loving ourselves from outside ourselves. The way I do this is by imagining watching myself in a movie. It is a technique which requires a little practise but is quite exciting once you are able to do it. What it entails is the ability to imagine ourselves as a central character in the movie of our life. What greater story do you need to have a look at if you can see the story of your own life?

Try sitting back in a peaceful place where you are unlikely to be disturbed and turn off your cell phone, a difficult task these days! Lean back and be comfortable. (With a little bit of practise you will be able to do these visualisations on the go but initially it is advisable to try them in solitude.) Once you are comfortably settled, close your eyes and start watching the film of your life unrolling.

Imagine the film being presented by some big well-known studio and imagine your face looking out of the screen. Take your time. Initially you will find flashes of other movies entering your mind, mixing with the images that you are trying to see. Let that happen. Do not stress yourself, just go with the flow. Your goal is to watch yourself on the screen and to keep reminding yourself how much you love the image that you are looking at. Initially, look at what you think are your strong points and appreciate them. For example, if you think you have lovely hair see it shimmering and cascading when you move your head in a certain way. Look at how lovely you look when you smile and how it lights up your face. See how beautiful your hands are and notice how gracefully you use them.

When you are able to see this wonderful image of yourself on the screen it is easier to say 'I love you' to this person. Do it and keep doing it as many times as you can. There are no limits to the number of times you can do this and declare your love to this fantastic image of yourself. It is something that will change your life if you do it regularly. Just close your eyes and see yourself on that huge movie screen and say, 'I love you'. Do it for five minutes every day and see the difference after a week.

There are three key points to keep in mind:

1. DO IT. Most of us read these sorts of things, give them a perfunctory try and then forget all about them. We then convince ourselves we have tried this or that, but who has the time to do it regularly and, besides, it probably doesn't work, etc. Hence, it is essential to take some time out and do it the way I recommend you do it.

    One of the ways to ensure we are regular is to ask ourselves every night before we fall asleep the question: 'Have I loved myself today?' If the answer is no, then proceed to movie time for the last five minutes of the day before you fall asleep. Whatever happens, do try to practise this.

2. While doing this exercise, strictly keep away from criticising yourselves. Do not focus on anything that you think is negative about you. Initially this will be a little difficult as we all have a tendency to notice our shortcomings. The way to avoid doing so is to focus on everything we adore about ourselves. Train yourself to look for your strengths, not your weaknesses and make it a habit.

3. Let yourself go and see how much you can love yourself through this exercise. Remember there are really no restrictions to this. Given the way we have been taught to criticise ourselves, we cannot love ourselves enough. Do not restrict yourself in any way. Believe in yourself and think about yourself positively and it will become a reality.

This is one of the most powerful tools discussed in this book. Even if we practise this one lesson faithfully, it will improve our chances of not only finding our life-partner tremendously, but also improve the quality of all our relationships.

Week Eight

※

The SWOT Analysis

In the last chapters we talked about the things that we need to do to change ourselves in small ways. When we talk about a SWOT analysis (I will explain what it means in a minute) it is something that we all do anyway in some form or another. It does not require us to change ourselves in any way. Some of us do it in our minds, some of us do it instinctively and some of us may even write things down and analyse them before coming to a conclusion.

The first time I read about a SWOT analysis was in a marketing book. Essentially it is very simple and the four letters stand for the following attributes.

S   Strengths
W Weaknesses
O Opportunities
T Threats

Any product or person for that matter has some strengths and some weaknesses. For example, the man we are evaluating as our potential life-partner may have a beautiful, deep voice. It would simply be classified as 'strength'. He may be a very considerate person and again this would be classified as a 'strength'. On the other hand, if he is unwilling to be flexible in his thoughts, views or outlook it may be classified as a 'weakness' from your point of view.

We often talk about the above in terms of 'pros' and 'cons' and it really is one and the same thing. It is an evaluation that we do in our minds or in a written form before taking a decision. Though this whole process sounds a little clinical and analytical, we all do it. Some of us do this as a matter of instinct while some of us go through the process of actual analysis .

For the people who do this by instinct (also refer to my chapter 'Trust Your Instinct'), it is a lot easier. These people eliminate potentially unsuitable partners right at the beginning. They are now more or less ready to go ahead and get married. However, all of us do not possess this natural instinct or even if we do, we do not follow it. In that case, we might want to do a formal SWOT analysis before deciding whether or not to go ahead.

Assuming we are going ahead, we also need to understand what we mean by 'opportunities' and 'threats'.

Opportunities refer to the possible potential of the person with reference to the prevailing or future external environment. What it means simply is that if your potential life-partner is a finance professional and the banking sector is doing well, then he or she has a greater chance of prospering in his or her career. Another example, which might be relevant in the Indian context, is the number of people in the man's (especially the man's) immediate family. Depending on that, the situation could be interpreted as an opportunity or a threat.

To elaborate on the above, let's look at it as follows:

The guy may be mentally strong and while he respects his parents and siblings, he has a mind of his own. In this case, if the parents and siblings are well-settled and strong in their own right then the situation points towards possible opportunities wherein the family draws on each others' strengths for the good of all.

The converse situation is when your possible partner is a nice guy and open to agreeing with most things, that his family members say. In short, he cannot say 'no' to his parents or siblings. This situation is a possible 'threat' situation. It refers to the possible problems a person might face with reference to the present and future external environment. In this case it refers to the potential problems which women face in coming to terms with their future in-laws.

Essentially, the concept of 'opportunities' and 'threats' shows us a way to forecast how our future life-partner, with his or her 'strengths' and 'weaknesses', will fare in the game of life and especially with us by their side.

The question is, how does it help us?

Is it really worthwhile to think along these lines when we are blissfully in love with the person whom we intend to make our life-partner?

This is one of the most difficult questions that we face. In fact, I deliberated a lot before having this chapter here and the reason I included it is that I personally believe in the instinctive part of the SWOT analysis. I often do it when I am forced to evaluate people for particular roles or jobs. It is a sort of evaluation one does when forced to decide. I am not sure that I am always right especially because in interviews the time periods are awfully short. However, the time that we get during a courtship allows us to do some instinctive SWOT analysis and that is what I shall be focusing on here. For people who are interested they can create detailed SWOT analysis charts for which they don't really need this book. Just type SWOT analysis on Google and you will get some million hits!

How to interpret a SWOT analysis and what course of action to take after that?

A possible scenario:

You discover that the man you like has a roving eye, and is quite upfront about this tendency. What do you do?

You have two choices.

1. You walk away.
2. You love the person so much that you are willing to overlook this flaw and deal with possible infidelity at some point of time.

As far as I am concerned, any of the above choices are fine as long as YOU are comfortable with them. What I want to warn you about is the THIRD choice that a lot of people make and which is destined for failure.

The THIRD choice is the 'belief' that you will 'change him' once you get married. Maybe it does happen in a few instances. But my experience is these instances are fewer than we think. It is an onerous task to change people and if we are willing to choose our life-partner on the grounds that we intend to change them in the near future then we are definitely asking for more excitement than we might want to deal with.

Knowing how difficult it is to change people, this means we are already establishing unrealistic expectations in a relationship that may lead to trouble in the future.

I used to have a friend, who I met occasionally for a coffee or a film. She was a great person but she had a habit of asking for small favours that I found very irritating. Either it was money, or booking movie tickets, or taking a lift, etc. Though these were small things and I did not mind doing them, I realised that it was a habit with her to demand some favour or the other all the time. I am sure she had her reasons, and I am sure that some day someone would not mind it at all. However after a while, I began to be put off by her. Since she was only a friend, it did not really matter beyond a point. But I could not imagine spending a lifetime with such a person.

The point is, if you feel this way about your potential life-partner, you may need to rethink things before going ahead.

I have often interacted with people who are on the verge of taking a decision and have admitted to a couple of things they find unacceptable in their future partners and which they unerringly declare they will change after marriage. I am sure some of these marriages must have worked quite successfully for them. Therefore, the question arises again, as to how seriously do we take a SWOT analysis?

Personally, I trust my instincts and always enter into any sort of relationship, be it work or friendship, based on a clear understanding that I will not be able to 'CHANGE' the person. I may surely make suggestions and there is a possibility that a person may accept them and change to a certain extent (I have seen that happen), but it is not something that I would always bank upon.

When we think about a SWOT analysis, we often seem to focus on just the strengths and weaknesses whereas sometimes what we should be doing is focusing on the implications of those strengths and weaknesses.

Example 1: From a woman's viewpoint
If you perceive lack of height in a man as a weakness, then it is important for you to carefully examine its implications. Check out if the man is worried about his height and suffers an inferiority complex about it? If yes, then it may have a long-term impact on your relationship with him. However if he is not bothered about it and is a well-balanced person, then you need to re-check your feelings on the issue of height. Does its lack affect you to the extent where you feel

you have missed out on the Tall, Dark & Handsome package which you were promised since your teens? Is this weakness something that will have a majorly negative impact on your future with this person? If the answer is yes, it may not be a good idea to pursue the relationship. But if it does not bother you in the least, and all you do is give it a passing thought once in a while, then you can live with a weakness like this.

In a nutshell, it is important to assess the implications of the perceived weakness we think our potential partner has as shown in the example – from the viewpoint of both people involved and take an informed decision.

Example 2: From a man's viewpoint

A man evaluating a woman as his potential life-partner sees her tendency to try and control everything as a potential weakness. He observes this trait in all the interactions he has with her. She wants to choose the restaurant, the time, the mode of transport, the movie, and so on. How does this affect the man in the long run? As I have mentioned before, a lot of this depends on the man's personality. If he likes someone to take all the decisions in his life, then she may be the perfect match for him. Whereas if he likes taking his own decisions and feels boxed in when not allowed to do so, then the relationship is bound to flounder. The man here has to carefully evaluate whether he is ready to go ahead with the relationship or not.

The decision taken is based on an understanding of our future life-partner AND ourselves. Sometimes what may be unacceptable to one person may be quite acceptable to another and hence there may be no problems in that case. However, if we believe that we may not be able to live with the perceived problem then we might want to think things through before taking the plunge.

Love is a powerful motivator and sometimes such stuff may seem trivial. It is good to ignore it and go ahead provided you are willing to live with it without complaint. What should be avoided at all costs however is the belief that one can change another. Experience will tell people that this is a really tough one.

Sometimes there is a tendency to get bogged down with the SWOT analysis. For example, we may face a dilemma while trying to decide whether to go with the guy who is nice and straightforward but predictable, or with the guy who is good looking but unpredictable with a dangerous streak.

The best way to solve the dilemma is to think through what you really want and see what you are getting. In the game of choosing a life-partner there can be millions of possibilities. It is good to think about the big concerns that we may have and use them as sure-shot decision-makers. What I mean here is: trust yourself and your own judgement. After all love is one of the most powerful forces in this universe and it has the ability to surmount all types of obstacles and problems.

So go ahead and make your choice based on a broad analysis of the person's characteristics, your responses to them and your overall instincts.

Week Nine

Print the Cards and Send Me One

You are now ready to get married and I am expecting an invitation card…

Some of you may turn around and say that they are not ready to get married and I am sure there could be reasons for that. Some of the reasons could be:

1. We read the book in a few sittings in about a week.
2. Tried a few things but they didn't work.
3. It's difficult to practise all this … I did try one or two of the things but they didn't work.

4. Some things worked but I am still not married.

Answers 2, 3 and 4 were given within 2, 3 and 4 weeks respectively.

I am not saying that you need to read only one chapter a week and practise each principle for that duration and only then will you get married after nine weeks. The point I am trying to make is that IF you really want to get married within a FINITE period of time then you *need to take action.* I agree that ninety-nine per cent of us will read this book in a few sittings and probably casually try out a few of these things to see if they work or not. That is natural and there is nothing wrong with it. However, if you really want to get married within nine weeks, then you need to try and follow at least these four chapters that I am listing below.

Week One: Decide What You Want
Week Two: Make That Move
Week Five: Start Smiling
Week Seven: Love Yourself

This in no way diminishes the importance of the other chapters. It is just a reminder that these are four very easy things that you can do which will change your life positively and will aid you in finding your life-partner.

Of the above, deciding what we want, smiling and loving yourself, are all things that are relatively easy to do. I use the word 'relatively' carefully because I am aware that, for some of us, dealing with ourselves may actually be harder.

The fourth one, 'making that move' may seem daunting, but once practised, it can actually be very liberating. There may be a few initial disappointments which is natural. Continue loving yourself when such things happen and forge ahead in your efforts to make that move and it will bear fruit.

In essence, just reading this book will obviously not get you married in nine weeks unless you act on some of the things we have talked about. At the same time, for some of you it may provide help in a particular situation that you may be in.

Let us come back to the question of a person who has actually read this book and faithfully applied the principles. If after doing so, he/she has still not got married then all I can request that person to do is to keep continuing with these principles and rest assured that you will soon achieve the desired result. Sometimes it takes time to correctly apply these principles and sometimes it does require a little more time than nine weeks. I can apologise if it has not worked for you in the exact nine weeks and I can only wish that you meet your true life-partner at the earliest.

I would like to share a small story here about a woman friend who read this manuscript. She had been trying to get married for the last two years that I had known her. Since she was going through a phase where she seemed to have tried out everything possible she was quite excited to read the manuscript, especially since it related to her.

Though she made a lot of the usual noises about 'Yes I

like this' and 'This is exactly what happens', etc., nothing really happened with her own search. At least not till the next two days.

Two days later she came to me and asked me if she could borrow the manuscript again. This time she apparently read through it carefully and then within a week we met again. We met at a coffee shop and something about the way she looked made me realise that she seemed happier than usual. When I commented on it she explained that she was following the advice of the chapter on loving yourself.

'There is something in that chapter which made me think.' She hesitated and I could see that she was trying to articulate the many things going through her mind.

'It made me realise,' she continued, 'that for all these years I had never really allowed myself to let go and love myself. And right now I am trying to do that.'

We left it at that.

I had mixed feelings. Sure she was trying out one of the things in one of the chapters…but hey…she wasn't getting married!

When I met her again after three weeks, she was engaged.

She firmly believes that it happened as a result of her beginning to love herself more. She believes it made her more relaxed and more approachable, which allowed Manoj (the guy she is engaged to), to summon up the courage to approach her. If it was as a result of this book then I am happy. I am happier that things had worked out for her.

The above incident made me realise that for some

people even a certain part might spark off something which could lead to one thing and then another. This realisation convinced me that it wasn't really necessary to even wait for nine weeks for the final result of getting married. In a lot of cases it might even happen earlier.

I now address the majority of people who have read this book in a few sittings. I am making the assumption that while you have liked some of the ideas discussed here, you may have not had a chance to practise any of them. What I suggest you do then is pick any chapter from one to seven and practise what it says for the next seven days. Just try out ONE chapter for a week. Do it sincerely and faithfully with no sense of scepticism or doubt. Then see the results. If you like what you see, move ahead and try another chapter. If not, go ahead with your life and forget this book.

Some of you are now ready to get married! Believe me, it is a great feeling! It is getting ready for a wonderful life of love, respect, friendship and companionship. Go ahead and enjoy the feeling. All the things that we talked about still apply to our lives and even while making all the arrangements for your wedding do not lose sight of whatever you believe you have imbibed.

Some of you may be a little anxious about getting married and the last few paragraphs of this section are devoted towards addressing those pre-marriage jitters!

So your wedding is all planned, cards have been sent out, everyone has been informed, shopping is in full swing and yet you are a little anxious. A small voice keeps asking you, 'Are you doing the right thing?' For a few of you this may not be the case. You are blessed and should just go ahead and send me your invitation card. For some of you who are grappling with this last-minute doubt, you need to continue reading.

Most people fear commitment, especially a lifelong commitment like marriage. Even if they are in love, the very thought of having to spend the rest of their life with one person gives rise to doubt and apprehension. These feelings are enhanced given our modern lifestyles that have made us more independent, assertive and aware of our feelings. We are fearful of losing all those to matrimony. So how do we tackle this and the niggling fear of dealing with our future in-laws?

There are various ways to counter such thoughts and deal with the stress. For the sake of simplicity and ease, I will deal with one simple concept that I have found most effective.

'Be prepared for the worst, (then forget about it), and *then focus on the best possible outcome.'*

Let me elaborate.

Assume for a moment that you have got married and things are not working out with your in-laws. You are faced with the difficult task of confiding in your spouse about your dilemma and then maybe even convincing him to live separately from your in-laws. In the worst-case scenario, your spouse is unwilling to listen or empathise, and you are forced to go separate ways. In short, the WORST that might happen after marriage is the possibility of divorce. (I do not intend to deal with cases of physical abuse and torture which someone is willing to put up with. I am aware such things do happen but I do not believe that if you are reading this book you would have allowed yourself to get into a situation like that.)

Therefore, for a moment, we need to think about the WORST that can happen and tell ourselves mentally that 'this is the worst that can happen' and 'if it happens I will find a way to deal with it.' After all, divorce is not the end of the world and I am sure that in the most unlikely event it happens I will be able to deal with it.

That's it. All you have to do is prepare yourselves to muster all the strength to face the worst *IF* it happens. *Go through this thought process ONLY once!* Then it is important that you forget about it and focus on all the possible positive outcomes that you desire.

The above is just to help you face your fears once and for all. The objective is to reduce your fears to the minimum. You need to imagine it's like getting your new car scratched. In cities like Delhi and Mumbai it is very difficult to spot a car which does not have some sort of a dent or scratch on it. You have to be prepared for these few dents and scratches in the game of life as well. So be prepared for them but DO NOT dwell on them.

It is important to concentrate on two things here.

1. Be prepared for the WORST. But this is to be a 'one time' thing. Once you have mentally prepared yourself, you have to ensure that you do not think about it again. YOU CANNOT LET YOURSELF DWELL

ON THESE POSSIBILTIES. The reason I say this is because of the 'law of attraction' which states that whatever we think about manifests in our lives.

I have seen this happen in small and inexplicable ways in my early life when I did not have any comprehension of the 'law of attraction'.

I grew up in a small dusty town in eastern India called Dhanbad. We lived in large bungalows in the midst of coalfields and one thing that was common to all was the small domestic lizard that could be found scurrying around the walls and ceilings of these houses. It is not that I was particularly fond of lizards but at the same time I didn't really give them much thought. There was however a group of kids who were petrified of them and feared that one of these lizards would fall on them, especially the ones that hung upside down from the ceilings. And it did happen! Even at that time I remember noticing that it happened to the kid who was the most fearful.

One of my colleagues once admitted to me that despite taking so much care of her teeth she had huge dental problems and couldn't understand how people like me who were so careless about their teeth got by with minor fillings. I had felt even at the time that the problems we encounter are often a reflection of our worries.

Therefore, it is important to be prepared for the worst and yet at the same time not dwell on it. It may sound a little difficult at first but with a little bit of practise it works.

I use it in a very simple way at work. Once a year or once in a while I ask myself, 'What is the worst that could happen to me in my job?' The answer always comes back as, 'Maybe I can lose it.' Mentally I am prepared to lose my job any day if that situation arises. It gives me a lot of peace and the ability to perform my job without stress. At the same time I do not dwell on it.

What we really need to dwell on is the second part of what I had mentioned above, i e, *focus on the best possible outcome!*

We need to focus on what a lovely feeling we are going through now that we are getting married. We need to visualise and imagine all the possible desirable outcomes that would make us happy. This is the final key to our happiness – our ability to visualise our happiness and to believe in the positive outcome of these visualisations.

A lot of us tend to get very frazzled while making preparations for marriage and keep finding new things to worry about. There is nothing wrong in getting caught up with your wedding preparations but, at the same time, do not lose sight of the fact that you need to enjoy all the action and not get stressed about it.

An easy way to do that is to focus on the joyous aspects of getting married and then going on a honeymoon. The exact details and scale will be different for all of us. It may vary from a grand wedding and a month-long honeymoon to a simple court marriage and a weekend spent at home. Either way, it is a momentous step in your life and you need to visualise the elation you intend to get out of these moments.

So go ahead and dream up your perfect wedding, your perfect honeymoon and a perfect blissful life ahead. And one day, you will tell your grandchildren the story of how you found each other and got married!

Bon Voyage!

SECTION TWO

The last four sections deal with general themes and are not directly related to finding a life-partner but provide some interesting insights into the powers of appreciation, what parents can do for their children who want to get married, the effects of astrological predictions on trying to get married and finally how to remain married once we have taken the plunge.

10

✼

How to Use 'Appreciation' in Your Life

I f we look back on our lives we will find that some of our happiest moments have been those when we have received *genuine* appreciation. Think of the time when someone said something really nice to you and genuinely appreciated you. Try to recall that warm fuzzy feeling that stayed with you for quite some time afterwards. Appreciation feeds our soul, which is always hungry for appreciation, acknowledgement and understanding.

I have heard it said that a man can stay hungry for a long time, but wilts without appreciation. Appreciation motivates us to do things we would otherwise not do. Recent studies espouse the significant benefits of appreciating children in order for them to develop into well-rounded individuals.

A few years ago, when I visited Dubai, I got a chance to interact with dolphins. I have read that dolphins are one of the most intelligent species of mammals. Before I was allowed to go anywhere near them, I had a session with the trainers on how to interact with these amazing creatures. What they said was simple. Every time a dolphin performed well they were to be rewarded for their efforts, as this would make the interaction pleasurable for the dolphins as well. Appreciation, encouragement and reward mechanisms were the underlying principles of training them. It was interesting to note that when the dolphins did not respond favourably, the trainers simply ignored their undesirable behaviour. They did not reprimand or punish them.

What remained with me after this episode was the power of reinforcement of appreciation, be it in a human being or an animal. It is what we subconsciously strive for throughout our lives. Yet when it comes to appreciating people around us, we are somehow at a loss to do so.

First we have to be convinced that there is indeed merit in appreciating people around us, so that our praise is genuine. Then we have to figure out how we do it. We also have to fight our own belief of being *firmly convinced* that we do appreciate people around us, whereas in reality we fall short. What this means is that we often think if we have said 'good job' a few times to our colleagues it is enough appreciation. It is not. I will elaborate on this as we proceed. We also have to differentiate genuine appreciation from flattery.

All the above takes some time to understand, imbibe and then practise. What I will focus on are:

- The need for appreciation.
- How to make it a habit.

The rest of the accompanying principles will be explained as we work our way through these two major points.

The Need for Appreciation

I first learned about the power of appreciation about seven years ago. Once I was convinced it made sense I told myself I would use it. I used to travel around the country quite a lot during those years and once at one of the airports an opportunity presented itself to me.

I was walking into the Jet premier lounge at this airport and just as I was about to enter I saw Kamal Hassan, the famous movie star. He was leaving the lounge accompanied by one of Jet Airways ground staff. When I saw him, my first reaction was to stand and watch him go by. Then I suddenly remembered my promise to myself to appreciate people. The fact that Hassan was a celebrity and used to public adulation did not deter me.

I roused myself out of my comfort zone and walked up to him. I told him how I appreciated the concept of his film, *Hey Ram*, and his role in it. I could see a look of great humility and gratitude on his face. I could immediately make out that he was moved in some small way by what I had said. Emboldened by what I saw, I asked him for his autograph. He smiled and held out his hands towards me obviously expecting me to hold out a note pad and a pen or at least something that he could sign on.

To my chagrin I realised I neither had a pen nor a piece of paper. However, by then I was on a roll. Having embarked upon my mission, there was nothing that could hold me back. It was as if I was on auto-pilot. I looked around and noticed the lady from Jet Airway's ground staff who was accompanying him. I smiled at her and requested her for a pen. I could see her take in the whole situation in an amused fashion and then voila! she produced a pen.

I still needed something for Kamal Hassan to sign on and, in a flash, I had an inspiration. I held out my boarding pass! Within a few seconds I had his autograph and he was on his way. I watched them go and then sat down in the lounge with a kind of warm, happy feeling which is hard to describe. I was happy for three reasons.

The first two reasons were obvious. I was happy that he had so obviously liked being appreciated. It validated what I had set out to achieve. I was also pleased with myself for getting out of my comfort zone and actually 'making the move'.

It was however the third reason that was an eye-opener.

It felt good to genuinely appreciate someone, *irrespective* of how the other person felt. I had always known or assumed that people liked being appreciated. What I had not bargained for was the immense satisfaction the gesture gave me.

What I have written above sounds easy. It also sounds like common sense and yet we do not appreciate people as much as we should. I too fall woefully short of doing it frequently enough.

As I have mentioned before, I have worked in theatre. Anyone who has done theatre will vouch for the fact that one of the reasons for being in it is for our innate need for recognition and appreciation. I remember waiting with bated breath for people to come up and say nice things to me after a show. When they did so, it was far more pleasurable and memorable than the good news that came from the ticket-sales counter.

Everyone knows there is hardly any money in theatre, yet thousands of people, young and old, are in it. There is nothing that brings greater satisfaction to an artist than a genuine appreciation of his or her craft.

The need to be recognised, loved, acknowledged and understood is hardwired into our mental makeup. One of the best ways to observe this is in children. In their purity and innocence they demand it unhesitatingly from their elders and parents. Look at a child's eyes and expression when he or she does something and then shows it to you. See the way they react when you praise them. When we grow up, however, we tend to suppress these feelings in the same way we suppress many others. However, the need within us does not go away. It is always there and we cherish those moments when we receive appreciation.

It goes without saying that we are talking about 'genuine' appreciation here and not 'flattery'. This is a question I have often faced at workshops on 'appreciation'. The questions are varied: 'How do we differentiate between genuine praise and flattery?'; 'Even if I appreciate someone from the heart, could it not be misconstrued as flattery?'; 'What if the person takes it wrongly?'

My answer to all these questions has always been very simple. Appreciation is all about awareness. It is about being aware of the innumerable amazing things that are around us and which we tend to ignore. One of the simplest examples is the beauty of nature that is all around us and yet we totally miss it as we go about the business of our lives.

Similarly, there are hundreds of things that are praiseworthy in the people around us that we'd notice only if we had the awareness to do so. We take many things our parents, friends, colleagues and family do for us for granted.

One of the reasons we do not appreciate or acknowledge people is when we think that what they are doing is 'their job'. I have seen umpteen examples of people taking the smiles, politeness and helpfulness of the service industry people as their due, be it a front desk person at a hotel, an air hostess or ground staff, the hotel doorman or the bartender, whom we think is duty-bound to be nice to us. Even if it is their job, I firmly believe that it is our job to acknowledge them.

How to make appreciation a habit

This habit will not only help us in finding but also keeping our life-partner. Innumerable fights in marriages and relationships are caused by a feeling of not being appreciated enough.

So the question is how do we make this a habit?

1. Practise.
2. A genuine awareness on our part.
3. The ability to express our appreciation rather than keeping it to ourselves.

Think about something nice a particular person has done or achieved and tell her how much you appreciate her. Remember to think of something you genuinely like and appreciate, otherwise the person will know you are faking it.

Remember one thing. We cannot be appreciated enough. Some of us may read this and disagree. For them, my suggestion is, throw yourself into practising this. Once you do it and experience the results, you will feel the need to try it out again and again. That is how this becomes a habit. We have to practise. As I mentioned somewhere earlier in this book, it is all about moving ourselves to action. We have to go out there and make that move. Sometimes we also call this 'getting out of our comfort zone'.

It is so easy to get caught up in things and forget about the people around us. At the same time you will always find some people who are constantly generous with their compliments and appreciation. You will also notice that, these are usually happy people. They are the blessed ones who have realised that appreciating someone is tantamount to appreciating the universal consciousness which in turn means appreciating oneself.

Give a valid reason for appreciating a person. In ninety-five per cent cases, people tend to miss out as to *why* they are appreciating a person. People like to be complimented on their attributes and characteristics more than on their possessions or actions. It is, therefore, important to understand how to appreciate people before doing so.

What we are saying here is illustrated below with a few examples. The sentences in roman type are what we usually say. The sentences in italics are what we could follow these up with.

That's a nice shirt! *I really like the way you carry off your clothes!*

That was a good presentation! *You have a very pleasing personality!*

The food was great! *You really have an unusual knack for cooking!*

Your son is very well-mannered! *You have brought him up so well!*

Good job! *I like the maturity with which you handled the situation!*

Nice email! *You do have a way with words!*

In the second sentence you are taking the first initial round of appreciation (which could be sometimes misconstrued as flattery) to a deeper, more meaningful level. At this level you are appreciating the person's characteristics and qualities rather than just their actions. If you really think about it, this is the level of appreciation that we all really crave.

Just go out and look for things to appreciate and you will find them. All you need is an open mind and an open heart. Make it a habit to look for the good things in people. Focus on all the positives that you see in people and tell them about it. The result will be that you will see more of their good side.

As this develops into a habit you will see the change in people around you and then in yourself. When it becomes a habit you will find that all your relationships are fulfilling and less strenuous. The world will suddenly become a better place to live in.

Will all this help you find your life-partner?

It is a question I will leave you to answer.

We all love our children.

We have loved them since they were little babies and now suddenly they seem to have grown up and come of marriageable age. It is surprising how time has flown!

For some of us parents, all we want now is for them to get married and settle down. What we actually mean is we want them to have a happy and wonderful married life with kids (our grandchildren) so that they can live happily ever after. We also want to help them achieve this objective.

Some of us are happy if our children find their own life-partners while some of us may want to ensure that we are the ones who find them a match. There are also some of us who are fine with both the approaches. Whatever the approach, we are clear about the end result. We want that ideal match for our son or daughter.

How do we go about it?

In case you are reading this book and have read through the previous chapters then you are ready to proceed to the next paragraph. In case you have directly come to this chapter then I would recommend that you read chapters, 1,3, 6 and 8, which are as follows:

Week 1: Decide What You Want
Week 3: Trust Your Instinct
Week 6: Visualise
Week 8: The SWOT Analysis

The reason I ask you to read these chapters is because these four things will apply to your quest of that ideal match for your son or daughter.

You will need to decide what you want for them and you will need to trust your instincts while meeting prospective matches, with parents and relatives in tow. Visualising would help in making what you really desire manifest. Finally, a SWOT analysis would need to be done by you based on the final choices that remain.

Reading these four chapters will help you realise both

what should be done by your son or daughter as well as yourself. Now assuming that you have already read these chapters, the question is, what else do you need to do to ensure that your son or daughter gets married?

The most important thing I feel we should do as parents is to let go a little. We all love our children and are anxious to help them get the best in life. At the same time we need to realise the difference between us *getting them* the best versus *enabling them* to get the best for themselves.

One of the things we tend to think is that since we are parents, we automatically know better than our children. While this may be the case till they are about ten to twelve years old, once they become teenagers they pretty much think they know better than us. In some respects I also believe they do. By the time they cross twenty, my belief is they are much smarter than we parents think they are. However, this is a concept which is very difficult for us parents to grasp.

As parents we suffer from a relativity theory which is hard to forget. What this means is that our children will always seem to be children for us. Our love for them sometimes blinds us to what really needs to be done in order to ensure their long-term happiness.

We should try and enable our children to become independent. Once they are independent and able to take decisions for themselves, their lives and life-partners will fall into place. One of the biggest hurdles the younger generation faces whilst trying to get married is taking their own decisions.

A few days ago I was speaking to a friend of mine who told me that a lot of her friends did not go ahead in relationships with guys they liked because their parents were against him, and they were afraid that if they married that guy *what would they do if something went wrong?* Essentially, her friends were afraid to take decisions for which they would need to bear the consequences. While this may be more prevalent in India or certain societies for reasons which are beyond the scope of this book, it is a fact which needs to be dealt with.

What exactly are we talking about here? I will illustrate it with a hypothetical example.

Let us for a moment assume that Rashmi is in love with a guy. She likes him, gets along well with him and for all practical purposes he fits her bill of the person she thinks she wants to marry. As a parent, however, you feel that the guy she likes does not have that zeal or potential in him to forge ahead in life in the long run. You think he falls a little short of qualifications and the smartness required in today's corporate world. You see a picture of a guy who is nice and yet at the same time laid-back, falling below your expectations.

Enter Mr Perfect. You like him. Rashmi also can't find anything particularly wrong with him which might cause her to say no. You and your spouse, on the other hand, not only like this guy but you also like his family and are convinced that he will make the perfect husband for your daughter and the quintessential father for your grandchildren. What are we supposed to do now?

Let's look at this from the parents' point of view.

With our experience and knowledge of what our daughter is like, we sincerely believe that she needs to marry Mr Perfect. We believe it so deeply that we are willing to push her into doing so even if it makes her a little unhappy initially. We believe in our wisdom that it is all for a good cause and that in the long run she will be happy.

Now let's look at it from Rashmi's viewpoint.

She loves the guy, the ordinary guy and given a free hand she would go ahead and marry him. At the same time she senses her parents' discomfort as well as their preference. Her thought process might run like this: 'Assuming I marry Mr Ordinary or Mr Perfect, there is no way I can predict what will happen in the future. However, in case something does happen and things don't work out, I will have a better chance of taking it up with my parents in the case of Mr Perfect. Whereas, if something goes wrong with Mr Ordinary I am not sure how my parents may react. At the same time, I can't really pinpoint anything particular against Mr Perfect...I really don't know what to do!'

This is the dilemma that we as parents sometimes put our children through.

The objective here is to find a simple answer to a difficult question. I would also like to state here that in these matters there really are no absolute answers. What I put forward, therefore, are some basic principles which I believe we as parents should follow. I have observed these principles in a lot of relationships and have found them to hold true in most cases.

1. Enable our children to be independent.
2. Give them unbiased advice.
3. Assure them that YOU will be there for them even if they make mistakes.

Enable our children to be independent

According to me the first principle is one of the most difficult to follow. It requires a great amount of love and discipline to enable our children to be truly independent. It requires more than just blindly loving them and letting situations slide into phases where we are doing things for them and making them dependent on us or somebody else. It is a lifelong practise and yet it is never too late to start.

Every time we go shopping, my son clamours for a toy. On the occasions that we agree to buy him one, we often give him the money to go and make payments and collect his toy. His natural tendency at this age (he is six years old) is to be a bit shy. At the same time, he does go ahead and do it. In a small way we believe we are making him independent.

At the same time, I have seen teenagers being treated like kids by their parents. At an age when we were doing our own work in terms of filling forms for various exams and travelling to distant cities to take exams, I often find parents over-managing these situations with respect to their children. The point we need to remember over and over again is that it is good to love our children but at the same time it is essential we teach them to fend for themselves.

The animal kingdom is a very stark example of this. If a

lioness or tigress or any other predatory animal did not teach their offspring how to hunt, then very soon their offspring would die. It is a simple law of nature and yet sometimes we tend to cushion our children from the challenges they need to face in life by doing things for them. I have seen anxious parents trying to fill out forms for their children which, in my opinion, should be filled by the children themselves. I have seen parents trying to tell their children to do certain things which, I personally believe, should be a decision best left to them.

I am not saying here that we should not advise them. Only that we should not start doing things for them that they are capable of doing themselves. If we believe we want our children to think independently, we have to first let go of the notion that we know better than them. We have to acknowledge the fact that our children have their own thoughts, dreams and aspirations and that they can be on the right path despite our misgivings. We need to let go. We need to let them forge their own paths and not try to always tell them what they need to do. It requires us to step back and sometimes look at things dispassionately.

The moment we step back and let them feel the space you will find that there will be a tendency for them to come back to you. Be there for them, assure them that you love them, give them unbiased advice but let them know that the final decision in most things in life needs to be theirs. In short, let them learn to be independent. It is never too late to start.

Give them unbiased advice

What exactly do we mean by unbiased advice? It is advice that we would give any person who is not our son or daughter. What I mean here is that when it comes to our own children we often give them advice based on what we perceive are their strengths and weaknesses. For example, if we know that our daughter is a bit laid-back we may advise her not marry a particular man because he is very talkative and always in a hurry as we may feel that she may not be able to keep pace with this guy. Rest assured that the universe has its own ways of finding matches for various people and in a lot of cases the most unlikely couples share the most fascinating relationships.

Whenever we give advice to anyone, be it our children or others, we labour under our own biases and beliefs. It is something that is a little difficult to change. My objective here is not to change anyone's beliefs. It is to make parents aware that just as we have our own beliefs and convictions, so do most other people. We, therefore, need to keep in mind that we are all entitled to our own convictions provided we do not try to impose them on others. Thus it is important to try and give unbiased and fair advice to anyone who asks for it. The question is how exactly do we do this?

The advice we are capable of giving people is based on what *we* have seen and experienced in this world. Once we realise this we will also realise that there can be a different point of view for everything and that the number of viewpoints are as varied as the number of people that exist. One of the ways, therefore, to give advice is to phrase it by saying, 'My understanding of the situation is as follows…' or 'Based on my experience this is what I know…' or 'If I were in this situation this is what I would do….' There is no harm in sharing our experiences and beliefs with our children but we have to do so in an unbiased manner. We can tell them our experiences. We can tell them what we think. At the same time we need to emphasise the point that these are our viewpoints and as far as they are concerned it is up to them to act on it. It is their obligation to make an assessment of not only our advice but also anybody else's before they take a decision. However, the responsibility for their decision will rest on them.

Love your son or daughter unconditionally. Do not judge them, do not try to change them, do not try to lecture them, just love them the way you loved them when they were babies. Love them unconditionally despite your beliefs about them and despite your own beliefs about life. As you keep doing this you will realise that you are changing. Keep at it and slowly you will find that you are able to see things from your children's point of view. That is when you will be able to give them unbiased advice.

Assure them that YOU will be there for them even if they make mistakes

When dealing with our children we need to assure them that we will always be there for them especially when it comes to girls or young ladies who are taking the plunge.

This is not to say that young men are not prone to the

same anxieties. However, the expectation that they are able to take care of themselves even if they are alone is somewhat ingrained in society and a single man is somehow a more acceptable fact than a single woman. Having said that, even young men who are about to get married often need their parents' advice and approval. In some countries like India where the daughter-in-law often comes to live with the boy's parents, it is an important fact of life.

Therefore, it is essential that as parents we are able to assure our children that whatever happens, we will be there for them in case things go wrong.

We need to reiterate that we will not stand in their way of happiness and that even if they did make a mistake in their choice we would still be there to help them. All they need during these difficult times of trying to make a choice is love and understanding. Once they are assured that they can make a mistake they will be more relaxed in terms of taking a decision. Decisions taken like this are more likely to be correct.

Our job as parents is to help them reach this stage. The final decision has to be theirs. It is they who have to live with that person for the rest of their lives and it is important for them to be able to stand up and take a decision. They need to be assured that while they need to be careful in taking a decision they also have the right to make mistakes. In case they do they need to be assured that you will be there for them the way you have always been there for them.

I have heard stories of young women and men acceding

to their parents choices simply because they feel that in the event that something goes wrong, they can at least blame their parents. This particular line of thinking may serve some people but it is worth looking at an alternative to the above. The alternative is simple. It is the realisation that *we are responsible for anything and everything that happens to us in life*. We may blame others and find reasons for all the things that happen to us but the universal fact remains that we are responsible for our own life and the choices we make. Therefore, even if we choose to rely on our parents and trust their judgement over our own in matters of choosing a life-partner, then that too is *our choice*. Whether we blame them in case something goes wrong is irrelevant in the overall scheme of things since the ultimate responsibility is always ours.

We have covered the three principles that I outlined above, which deal with making our children independent, giving them unbiased advise and being there for them when they need us.

The last thing that needs to be covered is something that we as parents sometimes fall prey to. It is the phenomenon called 'what will people say?' It is a difficult thing to deal with. It would be easy for a lot of us to wish away this phenomenon, yet it exists in a very powerful yet unseen fashion.

We live in a society and therefore we have to acknowledge the existence of our friends, neighbours and relatives. They will talk about us and our children. Sometimes they may even berate us for not doing enough in terms of getting our children married. This is a fact of life and it cannot be wished away. In the big scheme of things this is something that is as old as our civilisation. What we can control however is our reaction to all this.

One of the ways to look at it is to understand that everyone means well. There may be the occasional person who is trying to be sarcastic but in general people mean well. In a way all they are trying to do is help. So look at what they say in that light and do not misconstrue what they say as an attack on your ability to get your son or daughter married. You have got to realise that while getting your children married is a great thing it is not something that you are obliged to do. There are millions of people all around the world who are getting married on their own steam with no help whatsoever from their parents. They are leading perfectly happy lives with no assistance from anyone.

We are not duty-bound to get our children married. Some of us have this belief that we are, and it is fine to continue with that belief. At the same time all I am saying is that we need not get bothered by what other people say about our efforts in getting our children married. Take it with a pinch of salt and get on with life. Get on with your search and get your children married at your own pace.

There is a reason I say 'own pace'. Sometimes I have seen parents pressurising themselves based on what other people are saying. Such self-created pressures are counterproductive to good decision-making and may lead to undesirable outcomes. Therefore, it is important to listen to people around us and to hear what they might have to say, but it is of paramount importance for us to take a decision based on our own judgement and our children's judgement. Do not let anyone else's judgement or actions cloud your own.

To sum up, the most important thing that we as parents can do is love our children. Love them and cherish them and all the rest will fall in place.

11

Astrological Predictions and Marriage

I once asked one of my friends why she was rejecting a guy whom she thought was perfect for her. She had met him through a family friend. He was settled in the US, but was willing to return to India, or stay in the US depending on what *she* wanted. He had all the qualities she was looking for, and *yet* she was not marrying him!

When asked, she told me that their horoscopes or kundalis did not match. Apparently, a couple of learned astrologers had advised her against the match. I will not go into the reasons, but suffice to say that this particular couple did not get together because of the astrological predictions that were tabled.

It took me some time to digest this. It would have been easy for me to pass it off as a one-off occurrence, but then I discovered that this was a major reason for a lot of potential matches to be called off in India. I also had to get my head around the extreme viewpoints that surround us regarding astrological predictions. On the one hand, there is an absolute faith in it, and on the other, an absolute disbelief in the whole thing. The objective of this chapter is not to examine this debate, rather to proceed with the understanding that the truth lies somewhere in between.

For the purpose of this chapter, we will assume that there is some truth in astrological predictions. It is important to align ourselves to this assumption if we want to make quick progress on how to align astrological predictions with our efforts to get married. For when we do that, we tap into the principle of the 'law of attraction' mentioned earlier. Meaning that, over a period of time, our beliefs become our reality – a self-fulfilling prophecy. Therefore, if we believe in the accuracy of an astrological prediction, there is a great possibility that we may actually see it come to pass. It is our belief that matters.

The simple question then is, how do we align the astrological data we receive each time we evaluate a potential life-partner?

We may come across innumerable permutations and combinations of scenarios.

For example:

1. We believe in these predictions to the extent that we can reject an otherwise suitable life-partner.
2. We are neutral about it, but our parents believe and are insistent that we follow the astrological advice they have received.
3. The astrological data might be favourable while the actual person does not seem right for us.

In short, there are various possible situations that we might come across. We need to find tools that will help us manage each situation with a view to securing a life-partner, i.e. how can we dovetail astrological predictions into our marriage.

What does one do when, on one hand, we like a person and on the other hand we know that astrologically we can never be compatible? It is a difficult situation.

We have our own beliefs and value systems that we need to acknowledge. Once we acknowledge these beliefs we need to prioritise in our own minds as to what takes precedence over what. As an example, let us consider something unrelated to marriage. Let us take the simple case of going for a movie.

When we are deciding to go for a movie, one of the first things that comes to our mind is the choice of film itself. We all have our own favourite type of movie. Some of us may like Hindi movies, some Hollywood movies and some of us may like other language movies. Other criteria are the cast of a movie, the movie theatre it's playing at, the timings, etc.

At some point we have to prioritise one particular criterion over the other.

Apart from those rare occasions where everything falls into place, we may need to prioritise what we want in order to achieve our goal. Getting married is very different from selecting a movie to watch, I agree. It is a much more serious business and requires a much more serious approach.

As I mentioned above, even with the non-serious business of watching movies (I apologise to the serious die-hard movie goers here), there are those rare occasions when everything falls into place i e, we get the right movie at the right time in the very theatre along with our favourite tub of flavoured popcorn.

Sometimes this will happen when we want to get married. We will find the perfect match and be astrologically compatible as well. If this is the case, good for you!

Can it happen to all of us all the time? Yes, provided we decide clearly on what we want and then positively visualise the same. If we are convinced in our mind of the ideal situation and if we are able to believe in it, then rest assured it will come to pass.

This is, therefore, the first approach where we need to be convinced about our own beliefs, prioritise all of them equally and then be ready to wait for that perfect match to arrive.

Practically speaking, the above will happen to some of us, while some of us may find ourselves struggling. In that case, we need to move to the second approach wherein we need to analyse what our beliefs are and then prioritise accordingly. It is important for me to state here that this is *not a compromise*, it is simply a prioritisation of our beliefs and I can assure you that the end result is going to be the same as above.

What do I mean when I talk about prioritising our beliefs?

It is a simple case of looking inwards and asking ourselves what really matters to us and why. We need to ask ourselves some really hard questions about what we want and more importantly *why* we want it.

The evaluation that we need to do is, do we like the person enough to go against an unfavourable prediction? Essentially it is a simple choice. Either we can believe in the power of the astrological prediction, and say a no to the match, or we can believe in the power of our own instinctive and rational judgement and go ahead.

We need to follow what we are comfortable with and what we believe in. Often, when we are in love with someone we may have a strong enough belief to ignore any astrological predictions. In fact, we may not even go for such a prediction if we don't feel the need to. This is absolutely fine as long as we are strong in our own beliefs. There may be instances where we like someone but are not willing to go ahead because of our belief in the astrological verdict and that is equally fine as well. Again, it is important to ask ourselves why we believe in what we believe. If we are happy with our belief then follow that. The end result will be the same.

Marriage is something which we need to be comfortable

about. Do not enter into a long-term relationship with any misgivings. Do not take a step unless you are absolutely comfortable with the same.

It is also important to realise that a great portion of these astrological predictions talk about compatibility, health, temperament of a person, etc. Some of these are attributes that we would also instinctively evaluate in our potential partners. In a lot of cases what we experience during our actual interaction with a person is also somewhat reflected in the subsequent astrological findings. If we let ourselves relax and focus our minds on love, harmony and compassion there is a great chance that all things will fall in place. There is an inherent sense of harmony in the universe which makes things fall in place for each one of us. We just need to calm down our minds and tap into this harmonious universe.

Essentially, this also goes back to the first chapter where we had talked about deciding what we wanted. In case astrological compatibility is an important point for us, we need to put it down in that initial list which forms the basis for what we really want. For some of us astrological compatibility is very important and therefore this needs to be an important point in the sentence that we create for ourselves.

In this case the sentence in the first chapter could read something like this.

I am so happy now that I have found this tall, good-looking intelligent guy from my community who has a great sense of humour and who is astrologically compatible with me.

This will keep us focused on what we want as the end result and once we are clear about it, we will find it falling in place.

I have personally known people who lead their lives based on astrological predictions and who are perfectly happy and harmonious in their lives. I have also known people who have never been to an astrologer in their lives and who are leading a joyous and fulfilling life without a care in the world.

As a footnote we also have the right to change our beliefs. What we believe today may not hold true for us tomorrow and we have full freedom to change ourselves based on what we hold true at that point in time. Essentially this is life. It is a place for us to try out our beliefs and thoughts and derive enjoyment from the same. In a greater sense there is no right or wrong in this world except where we are knowingly harming someone else.

To sum up:

1. Approach the concept of dovetailing astrological predictions into our marriage and come up with the correct solution for ourselves.
2. Depending on our approach, we need to incorporate it into our initial sentence right after we finish this chapter.
3. Wishing you all the best with your endeavour!

12

❋

How to Lead a Happy
Married Life

It might be prudent to think about how to ensure we stay happily married.

Before we start, it might make sense to dwell on what we call the so-called statistics of divorce or separation. The reason I say 'so called' is because despite my research, I found out that the statistics do not give us an accurate picture. At the same time, these statistics make us aware of the trends that are emerging around us. From one perspective, we could look at these figures and start relating them to our own situation. The other way to look at this could be to realise that getting a divorce in today's society is not a stigma anymore. It is not the end of our life and it is obvious that even after a divorce or separation, it is natural to get on with our lives. We can marry again, have further relationships and live the way we used to before we got married.

The reason I bring this up is *not* to advocate divorce or separation but to try and make the point that it is not such a big deal as it once was. Once we understand this, it will help us become a little more relaxed in decision-making. It is a simple case of preparing oneself for the worst situation and then proceeding ahead without any stress while expecting the best possible outcome. We often tend to take decisions based on fear. Meaning, we often take defensive decisions because we are afraid of the outcome. For example, when we are at work, we will often find that we are hesitant to speak our mind because we are afraid of offending people as then they may not like us and may make it difficult for us on the job or even cause us to lose our job. That is not something we want.

Therefore, in some sort of a subconscious manner, we tend to go through life without really letting ourselves go. For a moment if we were able to take away our fear of losing our job, we would find that we are able to function more easily and confidently. We will suddenly find that we are much more productive and valuable to the organisation. It is not difficult to do this. All it needs is a little bit of thought and the realisation that even if we were to lose our job we would get one again. We just need to believe in our own abilities and be prepared for such an eventuality. Note, in

99.5 per cent of these cases, this event will not take place and yet being able to face it will change our whole attitude. Observe people around you who have put in their papers and who are serving out their notice period in the company. You will see that they are more relaxed and are more able to focus and manage the things they need to in those few days. The reason is they are operating with a *free mind.*

Similarly, if we are always afraid of what will happen to our marriage it will not serve us well. When we worry about things and keep having fearful thoughts we are more likely to encounter them.

This brings us to the statistics on divorce. I will just touch upon a couple of figures which will tell us about trends, which is really what I am concerned about.

It says that given the current trends, the divorce rate in the United States could reach as high as 50 per cent. At present it may be as high as 40 per cent. India, on the other hand, has one of the lowest divorce rates in the world at about 1.7 per cent. However, and this is an important fact, the rate of divorce in all our metro cities have been doubling every five years and for a metro like Mumbai it may reach a rate of 40 per cent in the next few years. While this may sound alarming, it is but natural for us to catch up with the West as we have in so many other spheres.

One of the primary reasons is that women today have to a great extent become self-sufficient. It is possible for a woman today to live by herself. Society too has begun to accept the fact that divorces will happen. People are living happy married lives the second time around. The pressures of the modern corporate world are also one of the reasons for this. People simply don't have the time to bother about other people and hence a person who is divorced does not attract the undue attention that he did earlier. (This is only true for the big metros and that too in certain pockets.)

Parents too have come to terms with the fact that it is more important for their children to be happy than to stick to marriages that are crumbling. All in all, it is easier to be a divorcee today than it was earlier.

The point I am trying to make here is *don't be afraid* of the worst-case scenario that you can imagine for yourself – divorce. Do not enter into a marriage with any sort of misgivings. Don't worry too much about things which may or may not happen in future.

Having said this, I will now turn to the business of how we can prepare ourselves to lead a happy married life. Here are a few random points in no particular order which, I personally believe, are important for a marriage to be successful.

- *Your spouse is your best friend.*
- *Love your spouse.*
- *Take it easy.*
- *Do not harbour resentment.*
- *Listen to your spouse.*
- *Tell your spouse you love him/her.*
- *Do not crib about your spouse.*
- *Respect your in-laws.*

These are a few points which I believe are important for a joyful and happy marriage. Follow them faithfully and you will see the results for yourself. Again, just being aware of these points will not help, so practise them. I will leave you with some simple tips on how to practise these once you are married. If you are already married and you happen to be reading this by some quirk of fate then I guess you already know about these. So read on and check whether you are actually doing these things.

Your spouse is your best friend
One of the things that my wife and I enjoy is going to the movies. A Saturday afternoon will invariably find us in a mall with our six-year-old son in tow, strolling around aimlessly and enjoying the opportunity to chat and generally chill around. We love coming out of a good movie and then finding a nice restaurant to have a drink followed by a late lunch. This is generally followed by a browsing in a bookstore and then driving back home. It all sounds very simple, but I enjoy it tremendously. In short, I love hanging out with my wife. The reason this is possible is that apart from being husband and wife, we are also friends. We are able to talk about things the way friends can. To me this is one of the major reasons for making a marriage enjoyable.

If we can be friends with our spouse, we can rest assured it is something that will last us a lifetime. A lot of other things like the first flush of love, the initial sense of mystery and romance have a tendency to mellow down as we go through marriage. At the same time a true friendship is something that keeps growing and maturing as time passes by. Therefore, it is important to nurture this aspect of our relationship with our spouse. It is one of the key secrets to a long and happy marriage.

Love your spouse

While this may seem like an obvious statement it is the bedrock of any marriage. You have to love your partner. You need to feel the desire to be with your partner and take care of him or her. For those of us who have had a 'love marriage' (as we call it in India) it is already there for us to build on. For those of us who have had an 'arranged marriage' we need to work on it. We need to focus on all the positive aspects of our spouse and love them for who they are, without judging them or criticising them. We need to love them with all our heart and soul.

Sometimes, we may find ourselves angry at our partner. It is natural. At the same time we cannot let that anger remain with us. We have to explore ways to get over it and ensure we are giving out more love than anger. The more you love a person the more that person is inclined to love you. Do not get caught up in the game of waiting for your spouse to make the first move. Make the first move yourself. Giving love or making the first move for a reconciliation attempt, in no way diminishes your standing or status. On the contrary, it speaks about your ability to forgive and forget.

Love is the most powerful force in the universe. Give love

without holding back and see the amazing effect it will have on your marriage.

Take it easy

When I got married to my wife, I remember telling her a few days later that it wasn't as if things were greatly different. Yes, we were living together and having a great time, but it wasn't as if the world had changed. In our case, of course, we had known each other for a few years before tying the knot, but right before getting married we did have some apprehensions about our relationship post marriage.

Sometimes we tend to take things so seriously that we start worrying about possible situations which may never happen. The way to tackle this is to be relaxed.

In a lot of cases, marriage does entail a change of place, lifestyle, food habits, etc. Sometimes when we try to address all these issues at the same time and find a solution to all of them immediately, we may end up getting tense and worried. The art is to go with the flow. One of the best ways to go through the first twenty-one days of marriage (post the honeymoon, of course!), is to have a relaxed attitude with strong feelings of love and forgiveness.

Let's face it, some things will be different. At the same time different is not bad. Be nice to everyone around you and especially your spouse. Come Day Twenty-one and you will see that 95 per cent of the issues that bothered you are no longer there.

Do not harbour resentment

Resentment is holding a grudge against our spouse for something they did or didn't do in the past. While we may hold on to it and feel righteous about it, it really does not serve any purpose. Harbouring resentment is like holding a burning piece of coal in your hand with the intention of throwing it some day. It will only harm you and no one else.

If we find ourselves harbouring resentment we have two choices. If it is too profound and if it is something that we believe we really cannot change, then it is best to walk out of such a relationship. I leave it to each person to decide, based on what they think is the best.

If, on the other hand, it is not serious enough to warrant a separation, then we neeed to take positive steps to remove it from our minds. For this we need to understand why we bring up the same issue time and again. If we actually analyse it, we will find that it arises from a belief that our spouse does not care enough for us. A continuous belief in this will ultimately lead to this becoming a fact. Therefore, once we are able to identify this as a cause we need to share the same with our spouse. We need to make them understand our need for love and care, which are as important as food and water.

We must remember that love and care is expressed through actions and that our actions need to match our thinking. We may love our spouse dearly but we need to be sure to show it through our actions as well.

Listen to your spouse

In a normal situation our spouse is the person closest to us. She is the person with whom we share a great part of our life, bring up children and grandchildren, and finally grow old with. She is one of the few people who has the ability to truly understand us. Therefore, it is important that we listen to her attentively as this will allow us to understand what she is really saying. We will then be able to act accordingly and share a great relationship. If we do not listen, then we need to be prepared for the inevitable differences that crop up. On the other hand, when a spouse is confident that her better half is willing to listen to her, she is automatically reassured.

Sometimes, it is difficult to listen to our spouses. We will often hear the complaint, 'he or she does not listen to me'. There are some genuine reasons for that and it is good for us to examine some of these before we fly off the handle.

At home, we are in our comfort zones. We may be watching TV or doing something in the kitchen or reading a book, etc. We may become engrossed in it and if at that point in time our spouse chooses to talk about something profound we may have a tendency to miss it. If there is a genuine reason to interrupt your spouse, please go ahead. Otherwise, it would be prudent to choose the right time to say something that you want heard by your spouse. It is a responsibility that flows both ways and it is something that contributes to good listening.

Tell your spouse you love him / her

We need to express our love to our spouses directly, indirectly, through our actions and our behaviour. For example, tell her, 'I love you', send flowers, open the door for her, cook her a meal, hug him and praise him whenever you can.

I am also sure that if at this moment you just doubled all the above that you do, it would not harm you, rather, it will change your relationship for the better. The point is, not only can we not love our spouses enough, we cannot tell them so enough.

I know we often think about it in our minds and we know that we deeply love our partners. At the same time it is essential for them to hear it from us. There is nothing wrong with the strong silent type of love as long as your actions speak volumes.

Do not crib about your spouse

Have you ever had a great cribbing session with your friends about your spouse? Or for that matter even your boyfriend/ girlfriend? If you have not then that's great. Keep it that way.

If you crib about your husband's habit of snoring in a good-natured way, it's fine. If you crib about your wife's concern for you when you are late, it's fine.

However, if we are regularly cribbing about our spouses to other people, we need to stop. It is as simple as that. We need to understand simply that this will neither help us, nor our relationship. On the contrary, the more we do this, the more reasons we will find to crib. It will become a vicious cycle and by the law of attraction we will attract more situations to complain about.

Therefore, rather than cribbing to other people, we need to take positive action to solve the underlying reason which make us crib. Some of us may be in a situation where we firmly believe that there is no solution. We believe that our spouse will not change. We firmly believe that they are wrong. We believe that given our situation and the children (in some cases), there really is nothing that we can do. We believe that we are doomed to our present situation.

I agree that there may be some points in our life when we feel like this. I also agree that the advice here may seem far-fetched and relegated only to the pages of this book. At the same time, I would just urge you to change one of your beliefs, and that is the belief of 'things cannot change'. Things always change. So I urge you to start thinking about what you really want. I urge you to imagine the ideal situation that you would like and then focus on the same. In time, things will change. But they will not change if we continue to crib. So let's take a vow to stop cribbing.

I will also let you onto a secret. While we may love to crib, deep down we do not like to hear other people crib. After a point nobody likes someone who is a cribber. So make it a point to try and talk about nice things. Slowly you will see your life change. It is bound to happen. It is one of the secrets of a happy marriage.

Respect your in-laws

Our 'in-laws' are part of the package. They come with our spouse. We have no choice but to respect them. In a lot of ways they are like our parents. So respect them and be grateful to them that they gave you your spouse.

Remember, your spouse grew up with his/her parents. There is a strong bond between them. Do not try to come between that. At the same time it is important for both spouses to give each other the comfort that, all said and done, they are always there for each other and while they will both respect each other's parents they will also not allow them to significantly affect their lives.

As a spouse you need to know that your loyalty lies first with your spouse. This does not mean that you will disobey your parents or do anything drastic. It just means that you will let the world know that your spouse means a lot to you. It will automatically smoothen out things.

At the same time it is important for us to realise that there are many things we can learn from our in-laws. We must also realise that there are a lot of things that they might find strange about us. After all, there is a generation gap and we need to be cognisant of the same. We need to remember that one day we too shall be in-laws to our children's spouses and a lot of what they might do may seem strange to us. So be nice to them, respect them and do not look upon them as if they were from a different world.

All the above points contribute in some way to a happy marriage.

If you intend to get married then one of the things you can do is try and figure out how these things might pan out based on your current relationship. For example, will it be possible for you to be friends with the person you intend to marry? Do you like his or her parents? Do you like what they say?

A lot of these questions would have already been answered by you. A lot of these things are instinctive as well. So don't get too bogged down with things and go ahead and look forward to your impending marriage. It is a great event and it will change your life. Go forward with a positive mind and you will be successful and happy.

Due to circumstances, some of us may not want to enter into marriage, and want only a relationship. It may be a live-in relationship, it may be an affair, or any other such arrangement. All of these are important for the people involved and they draw upon all the fundamentals that we have talked about. Even in a 'live-in' relationship we need to love and listen to our partner.

Every relationship is important and the underlying principles that we have discussed in this book apply to all. When we want a relationship we need to decide what we want. We still need to take action. We still need to follow our instincts. In short, we need to try and follow the steps that we have talked about here.

Before ending this book, I would like to remind each one of you of an important fact: It is essential that we practise what we have read here. It is easy to gather information and consider it briefly in our minds. But, nothing will change unless we act on the information.

Now that we have finished reading this book I strongly urge you to go back to any of the first seven chapters and start practising at least one chapter. Just try it for one week in your life and see the difference. Take a leap of faith and just do it. I can assure you the results will be fantastic. Once you see the benefits of just implementing one of these chapters you will be encouraged to try out another one. Success begets success. After mastering two chapters you will find it easier to move to the other ones and try them out. Go ahead and make these small changes in your life and you will be surprised at the results.

As I have mentioned before, apart from helping you find your life-partner these chapters will help you in your day-to-day life. I speak from experience about all of these tools and I know that they are simple to do and yet they all have a profound impact on our lives. So go ahead and embark on this exciting and wondrous journey. See where it takes you and then move ahead from there.

Wishing you all the best!

* * *

www.ingramcontent.com/pod-product-compliance
Lightning Source LLC
LaVergne TN
LVHW021349080426
835508LV00020B/2183